P9-CMQ-407

BLAIRSVILLE SENIOR HIGH SCHOOL
BLAIRSVILLE, PENNA.

DISCRIMINATION

NATIVE AMERICANS STRUGGLE FOR EQUALITY

hundredfold   2/31/97   16.65

DISCRIMINATION

NATIVE AMERICANS STRUGGLE FOR EQUALITY

by
RONALD B. QUERRY

Rourke Corporation, Inc.
Vero Beach, Florida 32964

Cover design: David Hundley

Copyright © 1992, by Rourke Corporation, Inc.
All rights in this book are reserved. No part of this work
may be used or reproduced in any manner whatsoever or
transmitted in any form or by any means, electronic or
mechanical, including photocopy, recording, or any information storage and retrieval system, without written per-
mission from the copyright owner except in the case of
brief quotations embodied in critical articles and reviews.
For information address the publisher, Rourke Corporation, Inc., P.O. Box 3328, Vero Beach, Florida 32964.

∞ The paper used in this book conforms to the American
National Standard for Permanence of Paper for Printed
Library Materials, Z39.48-1984.

Library of Congress Cataloging-in-Publication Data
Querry, Ronald B. (Ronald Burns), 1943-
    Native Americans struggle for equality / by Ronald B.
Querry.
        p.   cm. — (Discrimination)
    Includes bibliographical references and index.
    Summary: Discusses the effect discrimination has had
and continues to have upon Native American peoples.
    ISBN 0-86593-179-8 (alk. paper)
    1. Indians of North America — Government relations —
Juvenile literature.   2. Indians of North America —
History — Juvenile literature.   3. Discrimination —
United States — Juvenile literature.   [1. Indians of North
America — History.   2. Discrimination.]   I. Title.
    II. Series.
E93.Q47   1992   92-7474
973'.00497 — dc20   CIP
                                                   AC

CONTENTS

DISCRIMINATION

NATIVE AMERICANS STRUGGLE FOR EQUALITY

1 What Is Discrimination?

This book is one in a series of works dealing with discrimination, and while we will be concerned in the present volume with the effect discrimination has had and continues to have upon Native American peoples, it is important that we begin by establishing a basic understanding of the more general concepts which we will be discussing as well as the terms we will be using so that we might better understand the very nature of discrimination and some of the forms it takes.

Prejudice and Discrimination

The term *discrimination*, taken by itself, is not always a negative term. To discriminate can and often does mean to make clear or fine distinctions. A person who has the ability to see or make these fine distinctions is said to be discriminating. For our purposes here, however, we will be using the term discrimination in its meaning as behavior that often occurs as a result of prejudice.

Prejudice is an *attitude* — an adverse judgment or an opinion formed beforehand or without knowledge or examination of the facts. Prejudice can be directed toward any group and may be based upon any number of attributes including age, occupation, social class, or region of residence. Most commonly, however, prejudice is based upon *ethnic* characteristics — that is, race, religion, language, national origin, and cultural traditions — or upon sex.

There are several theories having to do with how it is that people come to be prejudiced. Many experts agree that most of our prejudices are learned — that is, learned from our parents, from our friends, and from our culture. Clearly the prejudices that our parents display as we are growing up will be learned, and so it's not surprising that we are likely to adopt as our own the prejudices of our parents. Later on in life, we tend to adjust our attitudes — and thus our prejudices — according to how we perceive the attitudes of our peer or reference groups. Which is to say, we measure the *correctness* of our attitudes against those held by the group with whom we most identify.

Important, too, in learning prejudice, is the way in which certain groups are portrayed in the popular media — television, motion pictures, and so on. As early as 1950 sociologists were noticing that audiences of motion pictures and television tend to accept as true that part of a movie or TV story which is beyond their experience — that is, if some theater audience had never seen, say, a black person and sees that person portrayed on the screen as a dim-witted, slowmoving, lazy, and irresponsible individual, then it follows that audience might well believe that to be an accurate portrayal of *all* black people. During World War II, even Disney cartoons portrayed Japanese characters as evil, nearsighted, buck-toothed demons who spent most of their days torturing innocent people, and Germans as giant baby-eating "Huns"; it is easy to see how prejudice against these groups was reinforced by such images. This idea of how groups are portrayed as entertainment is especially relevant to our later focus on Native Americans, and we will examine it more closely in Chapter 7.

Other causes of prejudice include *intergroup rivalry* and economic factors. In intergroup rivalry we see that when different ethnic groups live in close proximity and must compete for resources — land, water, etc. — they may come to feel threatened each by the other and so form attitudes of dislike and prejudice

War and Pestilence!

HORRIBLE AND UNPARALELLED
MASSACRE !

Women and Children

FALLING VICTIMS TO THE

INDIAN'S TOMAHAWK.

While many of our most populous cities have been visited by that dreadful disease, the Cholera, and to which thousands have fallen victims, the merciless Savages have been as fatally engaged in the work of death on the frontiers; where great numbers (including women and children) have fallen victims to the bloody tomahawk.

Indians who were defending their homeland and their way of life were stereotyped as savage murderers. (Library of Congress)

and ultimately discriminate against one another. We will see an example of this kind of intergroup rivalry when, in Chapter 8, we discuss the Navajo and Hopi land disputes in Arizona.

Prejudice that results from *economic factors* differs somewhat from other prejudice in that while the prejudice is generally directed against a particular ethnic group, it is based almost solely upon economic factors — the feeling that one group's jobs (and thus its standard of living) are threatened by another group.

The term *scapegoat* is used when an object — object being a person or group — of prejudice and discrimination exists as a substitute for the real source of frustration or discontent. Readily identifiable ethnic groups are often chosen as scapegoats — for example, when jobs are scarce, the blame might be placed on "cheap Mexican labor" when in fact it is a downswing in the economy that is the cause. In such cases aggression has been misplaced onto a highly visible and relatively powerless group.

Forms of Discrimination

It has been suggested that discrimination can occur where there is no established prejudice. The example of this type of discrimination is said to be found in *colonialism*, wherein one country enters or invades another for the purpose of seizing the resources of the overpowered country. Some authorities maintain that when colonialism occurs, the discrimination comes first and that the prejudice comes only later.

Discrimination takes many forms. Clearly, the ultimate discrimination is *genocide* — the deliberate and systematic murder of a racial, political, or cultural group. The most often cited example is the Holocaust: the slaughter of Jews carried out by the Nazis (the National Socialist German Workers' Party) in the Third German Reich from 1933 to 1945 under Adolf Hitler. The Nazis believed that Germans were members of a superior race and that Jews and other "inferior" groups should be eliminated or enslaved. As a result of this *racism*, more than six million Jews were murdered.

Other examples of genocide in the twentieth century include the Turkish government's killing of at least a million Armenian people in 1915 in its attempt to rid Turkey of all Armenians; the government of Pakistan killing between one to three million Bengalis in 1971; and, more recently, the killing of an estimated one to three million Kampuchean people by the Khmer Rouge between 1975 and 1979 — Kampuchea has since come to be known by some as "The Killing Field."

It's sad to say, but the government of the United States of America is not without its own dark history of genocide. As we will see in Chapter 4, an official policy of extermination of Native Americans was in fact in place and carried out to no small degree during the late 1800s in this country.

Less final than genocide certainly, but tragic nonetheless, are the many other forms which discrimination may be said to take.

Sexism is discrimination that occurs as a result of negative attitudes (prejudice) toward people because of their biological sex. Most often this type of discrimination is economic; that is, the discrimination is carried out in terms of an individual's opportunities for employment (and, once employed, advancement), and in wages paid to employees according to their sex. And while sex discrimination can be directed against males as well as females, it is women who have historically been the victims of sex discrimination. For example, the most recent figures available show that while women make up 40% of this country's work force, a female worker earns slightly more than half the salary of her male counterpart. This is discouraging when viewed within the context of the Civil Rights Act of 1964, which prohibits discrimination against women in employment.

Homophobia is what occurs when there exists an unreasoning fear or suspicion of people because of their sexual preference. Gay men and women are often the victims of discrimination.

Segregation is the separation or isolation of groups of people by custom or by law. Most often segregation is based upon race, class, or ethnic group and may be seen to occur in most areas of life. It is most readily observed in the areas of employment, housing, and education.

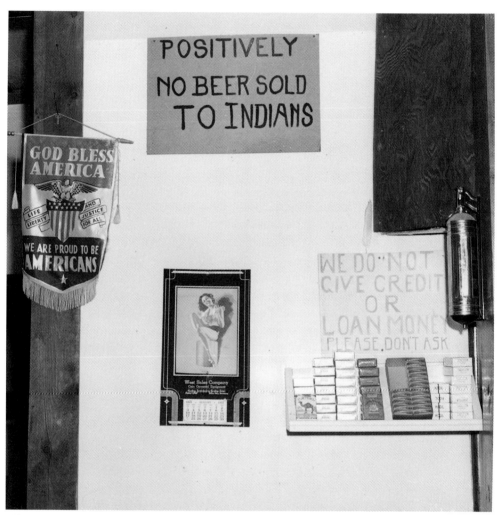

Blatant discrimination against Indians was common in the West, just as it was against blacks in the segregated South. (Library of Congress)

It should be noted that most forms of discrimination are prohibited by law in the United States. The 1964 and 1968 Civil Rights acts passed by Congress prohibit not only discrimination against women in the workplace, as mentioned above, but also discrimination by race — as well as other considerations — in employment, public accommodations, and in housing.

The World is Our Neighborhood

Discrimination is not a modern phenomenon. In fact, it is unlikely that there has ever been a race or a culture or a religion that has not felt or displayed discrimination. The attitudes people have toward discrimination have come about over time mostly due to the evolution of mass communication — the fact that the world is a "smaller" place than it has been at any other time in history. By "smaller" we mean to suggest that with television and the electronic transmission of photographs that bring world events into our homes as soon as they occur, we have in fact become a world community. No longer can we look at far away countries and the events that are occurring within them as distant and mysterious. Rather we have come to look upon the world as our neighborhood and to recognize that when any people suffer persecution, prejudice, or discrimination, the suffering of those people touches all of us.

If we are to eliminate or significantly reduce prejudice and discrimination, it will take enormous effort by people — all people — of every race, of every color, and of every culture and religion.

TERMS AS USED IN THIS DISCUSSION

Attitude: a feeling or emotion toward a group
Bigotry: strong prejudice, especially in matters of race, religion, and politics; intolerance of differing attitudes

Colonialism: control by one power over a dependent area or people

Discrimination: prejudiced outlook, action, or treatment

Ethnic: a group of people classed according to customs or common traits — language and social views, for example

Genocide: the systematic, planned annihilation of a racial, political, or cultural group

Homophobia: unreasoning fear of or antipathy toward homosexuals and homosexuality

Prejudice: irrational suspicion or hatred of a group, race, or religion

Racism: the idea that one's own race is superior to another

Scapegoat: a person or group that bears blame for others

Segregation: the separation of groups of people by law or by custom

Sexism: prejudice or discrimination against a person or group based on the biological sex of that person or group

Stereotype: An overly simplified and inaccurate view that all members of a particular group hold identical beliefs and conform to the same way of behavior

2 The Native American Experience

Native Americans is the term that is used to describe those people who are, in fact, native to the so-called "New World" that Christopher Columbus stumbled upon during his infamous voyage five hundred years ago. In 1492, Columbus mistakenly believed that he had landed in the region then known as the Indies — and thus he bestowed the name "Indians" upon the people he found to be living there.

Archeologists believe that the earliest ancestors of the Native peoples of North America first began to cross from Asia to what is now Alaska some 45,000 years ago — across a land bridge where the Bering Strait is today. Over the next several centuries, these peoples migrated southward across what we know today as Canada, the United States, Mexico, Central America, and South America.

While it's important that we recognize that authorities believe that those tribes and peoples that we have come to know as Native Americans are descended from the same ancestors as are the Indian peoples in Canada and Mexico as well as those in Central and South America, our concern here is limited to the area included within the borders of the United States, and so it is that area that will be the focus of this book.

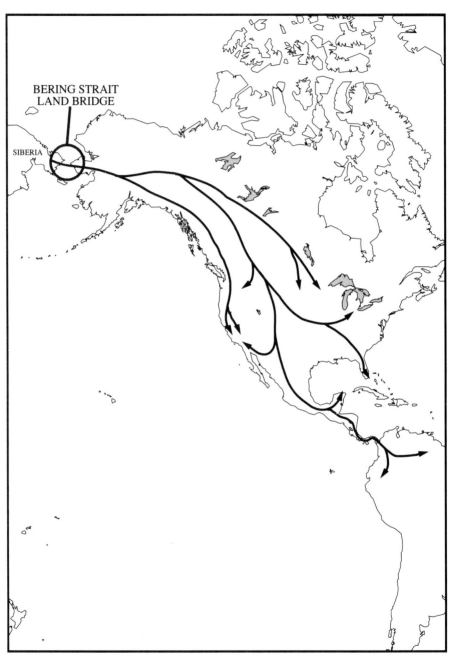

How the Ancestors of Native Americans Populated the Continent

The Arrival of Europeans

The arrival in the sixteenth century of the white man — or, more precisely, the *non-Indian* — caused a great disruption to the way of life of the gentle people already living here. The unintended yet deadly introduction of diseases that were heretofore unknown had an immediate and devastating effect on the natives. The early colonists in America — many if not most of whom were Christian zealots — caused dismay among the natives by destroying their religious sites and icons, and insisting that they believe and behave in the manner of the non-native intruders.

During the seventeenth and eighteenth centuries there took place a great struggle between the British and the French for supremacy both in Europe and in colonial America. Earlier on, both sides had discovered that they needed the cooperation of the Native people if they hoped to survive. Up until the time of the Seven Years' War (1756-1763), the Indians had for the most part thrown in with the French, but British reinforcements made the Redcoats a formidable foe, and by the end of the war the British had become the masters of North America. It was then that there occurred one of the earliest attempts by the conquerors to exterminate the Native population. Soldiers from Fort Pitt, at what is now Pittsburgh, Pennsylvania, distributed contaminated blankets to the Delaware Indians — blankets that had intentionally been taken from the British smallpox hospital — and the epidemic that resulted essentially wiped out the peaceful Delaware Tribe. Because of their experience with the Indians, the British had determined that there was to be no expansion west of the Appalachians. During the War of Independence however, the colonists renewed their push to the west, engaging and killing Native people as they went.

It wasn't long before white traders appeared among western tribes, and with them they brought trade goods, whiskey, and disease. Once again, in 1837, an entire tribe — this time the

Mandan Tribe of the Northwest — was wiped out by smallpox. Whether this was, as in the case of the Delaware Tribe, a case of intentional infection by the British is not particularly significant in light of the fact that prior to the introduction of the disease by European intruders, smallpox was unknown on this continent.

Navajos in Canyon de Chelly; in 1864, Kit Carson attacked the Navajos here. (Elaine S. Querry)

Removal

The growing population of white settlers east of the Mississippi River increased rapidly during the early part of the nineteenth century in the territory that then formed the central and southern United States. But this territory was already occupied by tribes of Indians who had always lived there. And so another dark day in this country's treatment of its Native people came on May 28, 1830, when Andrew Jackson's Removal Bill was enacted into law by Congress. According to this bill, most of the Southeastern tribes were forcibly removed from their homelands and made to relocate west of the Mississippi, mostly to the newly established Indian Territory — the eastern half of what is now Oklahoma — a territory that the government promised would remain Indian lands for all time, never to become a part of any state or the United States.

Most affected by the Removal were the Five Civilized Tribes — the Choctaw, the Chickasaw, the Cherokee, the Creeks, and the Seminoles. First to be moved (in the Fall of 1831) were the Choctaw of Mississippi, who eventually lost one out of every four of those who started the long journey from their Mississippi homeland to Indian Territory. It was the later removal of the Cherokee that gave the name Trail of Tears to the Removal — for the Choctaw people, it was the Long Sad Walk. When the Civil War broke out in 1861 the Five Civilized Tribes first offered to fight on the side of the Union but were turned down because they were "savages." While some Indian regiments fought on behalf of the armies of both the North and the South, the greater number of Indians of the Five Civilized Tribes took the side of the Confederacy.

By the end of the Civil War in 1865, there were 400,000 white settlers occupying that area between the Missouri and the Rocky Mountains — twice as many as there were Native people. With Union victory, much of the Indians' land was again taken from them — treaties that had promised the Indians land that would be theirs forever were snatched away as soon as white settlers determined that they wanted additional land. By the turn of the century, the Indians had been dispersed and there were upwards of one and a half million whites dominating the area.

The Indian Wars

During the years of the Civil War there were battles waged not only between the armies of the North and South but also between

Sitting Bull. (Library of Congress)

George Armstrong Custer. (Library of Congress)

the government and the Native people. In 1864 the Colorado Volunteers, led by Colonel John Chivington, attacked the peaceful Cheyenne camps of Black Kettle and White Antelope and killed 133 Indians — 105 of whom were women and children — at what has come to be called the Sand Creek Massacre. Survivors of this tragedy related how the soldiers shot children as young as five and how they scalped and otherwise mutilated the bodies of the Indians.

Three years later, in 1867, George Armstrong Custer, then a Colonel under the command of General Philip Sheridan, attacked Black Kettle's camp on the Washita River in Oklahoma, killing ninety-two women and children and eleven warriors. History records that it was Sheridan who first spoke those awful words that were later to become the motto of John Wayne and other Hollywood "Indian fighters": "The only good Indians I ever saw were dead." Custer, of course, met his own death at the hands of Sitting Bull and the Sioux at the Little Bighorn in 1876.

In the Southwest, in Arizona and New Mexico as well as further south into Mexico, the Apache Wars were carried out against the great warrior chiefs Mangas Coloradas, Cochise, Victorio, and Geronimo. To the north, in the Rocky Mountains, the Utes had already signed away all of Colorado east of the Continental Divide for $100,000 worth of supplies to be doled out over a ten-year period. The whites would not be satisfied, however, until they had all of the Utes' homelands and had driven all the Native people from the territory. The U.S. government moved the Utes to Utah, and by 1881 the whole of Colorado belonged to the white man.

On the Pacific side of the Rocky Mountains, in what is now Idaho, Oregon, and Washington, the Nez Perce, under the leadership of Chief Joseph, fought hard to keep their lands but in 1877 were defeated and sent to Fort Leavenworth in Kansas. Then, in the late 1800s there appeared the Paiute Messiah, Wovoka, who told the people that the end of the white man was at hand and taught them to dance the Ghost Dance. He claimed that for each white man that died, a buffalo would be born, and that by wearing the Ghost Shirts, warriors could not be harmed by the white man's bullets. When he had first heard of this new religion, Sitting Bull, the Sioux chief who had defeated Custer at the Little Bighorn, asked the Indian Agent if he might go and study it, but was refused. Later a Sioux Medicine Man called Kicking Bear visited the Standing Rock Agency and taught the Ghost Dance to Sitting Bull, who quickly accepted the new faith. When he announced in December of 1890 that he intended to leave the reservation, Sitting Bull was shot and killed as he sought to avoid arrest by the 43 Indian police sent by the Indian Agent to apprehend him.

Within two weeks of Sitting Bull's death, U.S. Army troops surrounded the camp of Big Foot and his followers at Wounded Knee near the Pine Ridge Agency. In all, some 180 Sioux were killed and wounded. The Indians had earlier surrendered their arms and were simply slaughtered by the soldiers. According to one survivor, Louise Weasel Bear, "We tried to run, but they shot us like we were buffalo."

Government Policy and the "Indian Problem"

The massacre at Wounded Knee, South Dakota, on the 28th of December 1890, marked the end of the Indian Wars. Still, the United States government viewed the very fact of Native Americans as a problem, and throughout the first half of the twentieth century, the government made several attempts to solve what it saw as the "Indian problem." In 1887 there was enacted a law whereby it became possible to break up the existing reservations and to divide them into *allotments*. This act — the *Severalty Act*, as it was known — would take the lands that had been given to a tribe as their new homeland and divide it into tracts that were then assigned to individual members of that tribe. In fact, however, the plots of land that were assigned to tribal members would never include all of the reservation, and that surplus, or "unassigned" land, would then be opened to white

Many Indians continue to prefer the wide-open spaces to the crowded life of the city. (Arnie Rosner/Photobank)

settlement. In addition, oftentimes the Native people—unaccustomed as they were to land ownership—easily fell victim to unscrupulous land dealers and developers who literally stole the land from the Indians by the act of buying it for ridiculously low prices.

It wasn't until 1924 that Congress granted citizenship to all Indians, and then at least one tribe—the Iroquois—sent word to the United States that they weren't at all interested in being citizens, thank you very much. To this day the Iroquois have not wavered from that stand.

The 1920s marked another particularly dark period in the history of Native American people. The death rate among Indians during that decade far exceeded the birth rate—it was as though Native peoples really had become an endangered species.

Then came the Indian Reorganization Act of 1934, which prohibited further allotment of lands and in fact appropriated monies annually for the future acquisition of new Indian lands. By the end of World War II, however, all thoughts of reform seem to have vanished as non-Native developers, businessmen, and farmers began once more to cast greedy eyes on Indian lands.

During the 1950s there was officially adopted a policy toward the Native population of termination—termination, that is, of tribal self-rule and government. States were given the power to extend their control over Indian reservations—to terminate all forms of tribal self-government—and it was not until 1968 that yet another bill was passed that required the Indians to give their consent to such control. During this dark period some sixty-one tribes lost their federal support.

The Native American Community Today

The term Native American must be viewed keeping in mind the wide diversity of peoples that term encompasses. Today there are more than 300 Federally recognized tribes and bands of Native Americans operating out of some 285 Tribal offices in all 50 states and the District of Columbia. According to the 1990 Census, the Native population of the United States is 1,878,000—and half of that population resides in five states: Oklahoma, California, Arizona, New Mexico, and Alaska. The Navajo Nation is, by far, the largest tribal group in the United States with a population of 143,400, and the Cherokee, Creek, Choctaw, and *Tohono O'odham* Tribes make up the remainder of the five largest.

If the fact that there are more than three hundred tribes and a total population of nearly two million appears, at first glance, to be a sign of health and prosperity, we will learn in the following chapters that the number of native people occupying North America when Columbus first visited has been estimated at upwards of fifteen million. We will see that the policies of extermination and subjugation of Native Americans continued long after this country was considered settled and civilized. And we will examine some of the problems that have resulted in a 1991 report by the Native American Alliance that suggests fully two-thirds of the Native American population in this country is living in poverty, one third is illiterate, and nearly ninety percent depends on government assistance.

Indian Populations of the Ten States with the Largest American Indian Populations, in thousands

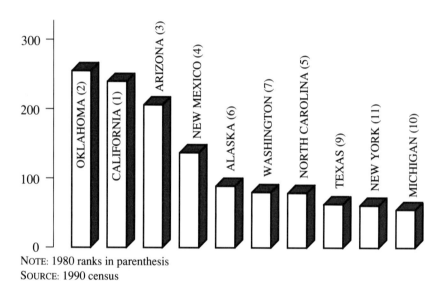

NOTE: 1980 ranks in parenthesis
SOURCE: 1990 census

I, in order that they might be very friendly towards us, because I knew that they were a people who could better be freed and converted to our Holy Faith by love than by force, gave to some of them red caps, and glass beads which they hung on their necks, and many other things of small value, in which they took so much pleasure and became so much our friends that it was a marvel.

Christopher Columbus, 12 October 1492

All he could see were naked, red-skinned savages. They threw themselves to the ground and worshipped Columbus and his bearded men. . . . They thought that gods had descended from the heavens. . . .

A children's book

Where today are the Pequot? Where are the Narragansett, the Mohican, the Pokanoket, and many other once powerful tribes of our people? They have vanished before the avarice and the oppression of the White Man, as snow before a summer sun.

Tecumseh of the Shawnees

No state or territory shall ever have a right to pass laws for the government of the Choctaw nation of red people and their descendents . . . and no part of the land granted them shall ever be embraced in any territory or state. . . .

Treaty of Dancing Rabbit Creek (1830)

Peace is much more fatal to Indians than war. A good season of measles or smallpox will accomplish more than all our troops under the best leadership. It is cheaper, wiser, safer and more humane to kill Indians with kindness than in warfare . . .

Helena Herald, 20 July 1876

[The white man] made us many promises, more than I can remember, but they never kept but one. They promised to take our land, and they took it.

Red Cloud, Dakota Sioux

The aim of legislation for the Indian should be to make him as soon as possible an intelligent, useful citizen.

17th Annual Report of the Board of Indian Commissioners (1885)

"The only good Indians I ever saw were dead."

General Philip Sheridan

"The whites are crazy!"

Arapaho Ghost Dance Song (1890)

On June 2, 1924, Congress conferred citizenship on all Indians born in the United States. . . . Since then they have possessed the same rights, privileges, and obligations as other citizens.

> Report of the Commission on the Rights, Liberties, and Responsibilities of the American Indian (1966)

"Now you know how Native Americans feel!"

> Sign in the office of the Lakota Times beneath baseball team pennants for the "Pittsburgh Negroes," the "Kansas City Jews," and the "San Diego Caucasians."

3 Early Contact

On the morning of Friday, August 3, 1492, a flotilla of three small ships under the command of a Captain General who was known at that time as Cristóbal Colón set sail from Spain in search of new lands and, most importantly to the Captain General, gold. Ten weeks later — on Friday, October 12th — Colón stepped onto a beach and proclaimed it to be the New World. Neither this man nor those who accompanied him that day could possibly have imagined that this act of "discovery" would mark not only the period of expansion and colonization that they sought, but also the beginning of a terrible time of bloodshed and slavery.

For most of the five centuries since, the world has commemorated that event as the "discovery of America" by the man we now know as Christopher Columbus. Never mind that the beach where he first stepped was but a small island in the Bahamas or that the native people he noticed standing on that beach to greet the ships that day would have been astonished to learn that these sailors were their "discoverers" much less that the unintelligible words spoken by these strange-looking men no sooner than they were out of their boats were not a greeting, but rather a declaration by which Columbus took possession of the land in the name of the King and Queen of Spain. Never mind that this land that came to be called America by these intruders was certainly very well known to the millions of people who were already living there in 1492.

The Tainos: A Culture Destroyed

And how did Columbus view those native people who were there on the beach that day? Here are his observations, in his own words, from his *Journal*:

"They are very well built, with very handsome bodies and very good faces; their hair coarse, almost like the silk of a horse's tail, and short. . . ."

And then he writes, "They ought to be good servants and of good intelligence. . . . I believe that they would easily be made Christians, because it seemed to me that they had no religion. . . . I will carry off six of them at my departure . . . in order that they may learn to speak."

And later, "They are fit to be ordered about and made to work . . ."

And finally, ". . . they are of good stature, men and women, and not black. . . ."

Thus on the very day that Columbus "discovered" these handsome people of good intelligence, he divined somehow not only that they had no religion, but that they would make good servants! Then too he decided then and there that he would "carry off" (that is, kidnap and make slaves of) six of these gentle people so that they might *learn to speak!* The arrogance of the man is remarkable.

These native people, whom Columbus would later term *Indios*, were in fact *Tainos* — a people related by culture and language to the *Arawaks* of the South American mainland. The Tainos even then had a highly efficient agricultural system and a peaceful way of government and exhibited warm social relations with the Europeans as well as among themselves. Three months later, in January of 1493, there occurred what was probably the first battle between the natives and the Europeans when a group of Tainos refused to give over their bows and arrows to Columbus' men. It may well have been the first such battle, but it was by no means the last.

Shortly thereafter, Columbus and his flotilla returned to Spain. The first encounter with the native people of the New World was ended.

Perhaps not quite ended . . . for it appears that when he sailed, Columbus took with him as many as two dozen Taino captives.

As evidenced by his *Journals*, Columbus was the first to describe the native people he encountered in the New World as something less than human. Moreover, he was given to exaggeration of large proportions. For example, he reported that he had observed amazon women, people born with tails, and cannibals. These latter were believed by Columbus to be *Caribs*, whom he described as a fierce and warlike people. For a long time thereafter it was believed by the Spanish that any Indians who were submissive and peaceable were Tainos — that is, they

Delaware peyote ceremony; the European invaders did not understand Native American beliefs, dismissing them as "primitive." (National Museum of the American Indian)

were "good Indians." If, on the other hand, the native people showed any sign of hostility or attempted in any way to defend themselves against the intruders, it was thought that they must then be the cannibalistic Caribs — or "bad Indians." We shall see how this attitude has continued over the hundreds of years since and how it continues, to a lesser degree perhaps, even in modern times.

When Columbus returned to the New World on his Second Voyage, he came as Admiral of the Ocean Sea and as Viceroy and Governor of the islands and mainland of the New World — so appointed by King Ferdinand and Queen Isabella. And one of his first acts upon arrival was to institute a "tax" system whereby all Tainos over the age of fourteen were obliged periodically to bring a measure of gold to the new rulers. Since the island was not particularly rich in gold, this proved to be a near-impossible task. Nonetheless, those natives who failed to provide their quota of gold were punished by having their hands cut off and being left to bleed to death.

Española was one of the islands encountered by Columbus. Española is the Spanish name (sometimes Anglicized as "Hispaniola") of that relatively small island in the heart of the Caribbean that is today divided into what we know as the Republic of Haiti and the Dominican Republic. The original, indigenous, name of the island — *Quisqueya* — is still used in the Dominican Republic as an "elegant variation."

While it's true scholars hold widely differing opinions on the subject of the native population of Española in 1492 — some estimates run to as few as 200,000 — there are modern historians who estimate it was just under eight million at the time of that first encounter. Yet twenty years later — due to disease and the depredations inflicted by the intruders — that population was reduced to some twenty-eight thousand natives. Fifty years after first contact — in 1542 — it was reported that there were but two hundred Tainos still living on Española. And soon thereafter the native people were extinct. This clearly was a case of genocide, perhaps the first involving Native American people.

Colonialism Throughout the "New World"

By the mid-sixteenth century the Spanish had moved to the mainland of Central America, where one monk reported finding Indians whom he described as "stupid and silly," "unstable," and as "ungrateful, brute beasts." Another Spaniard remarked that the native people he found "possess no science . . . lack letters and preserve no monument of their history. They do not even have private property" — certainly evidence of a lack of civilization, to not privately own property, indeed.

All during the sixteenth century Indians were kidnapped from the New World. And while the scope of the Indian slave issue clearly never approached that of the Negro slave trade, the fact remains: Native American people were sold into slavery in virtually every European nation.

In 1607 the first colony in what is now the state of Virginia was established at Jamestown. But rather than the story of Plymouth Rock (the English landed there in 1620) and Pilgrim fathers and Thanksgiving dinners, the establishment of the colonies in this part of North America signaled the beginning of a terrible history of prejudice and discrimination against the Native American peoples who occupied this land.

By 1610, just three years after the founding of Jamestown, the Virginia colonists were waging war against their native hosts in a most brutal fashion. One of the colonists described his 1610 attack on an Indian village in this horrible way:

> Then drawing my soldiers into battle . . . we fell in upon them and put some 15 or 16 to the sword and almost all the rest to flight. . . . My Lieutenant brought with him an Indian woman and her children and one Indian prisoner for which I scolded him because he had spared them. His answer was that having them now in my custody I might do with them what I pleased. Upon which I ordered that the Indian's head be cut off and then ordered my soldiers to burn all the houses and cut down the corn growing about the town. And after we marched with the woman and her children back to our boats my soldiers began to

complain because these had been spared. We agreed to put the children to death and did so by throwing them overboard and shooting out their brains in the water.

In March of 1622 Powhatan Indians — mainly because their lands were being taken away at an alarming rate — attacked colonists at Jamestown and other settlements, killing an estimated four hundred. The English colonists retaliated with an all-out war against all Indians of any sex or age. It became the policy to burn entire villages and fields and anything else that belonged to the natives. On at least one occasion, a group of colonists invited Indians to negotiate a peace treaty and, upon completion of the talks, persuaded the villagers to drink poisoned wine. According to one account, "an estimated two hundred Indians died instantly, after which the soldiers dispatched another fifty or so with more conventional weapons and 'brought hom parte of ther heades.'" The Powhatan War lasted approximately three years. It has been estimated that the Powhatan people numbered more than 40,000 when Jamestown was founded in 1607 and that there were probably fewer than 5,000 living when the war ended in 1625. Some sixty years later, in 1685, the English were able to report that the Powhatan people were entirely extinct.

In 1675 Chief Metacom, who had been "crowned" King Phillip by the European invaders, led a confederacy of Wampanoags, Narragansetts, and other New England tribes into a war with the colonists. The Indians found themselves being pushed further and further into the wilderness and went to war in order to avoid the extermination that was clearly planned for them as it had been for the Powhatans. They attacked many settlements and wiped out several. However, the native people were no match for the colonists' superior arms, and within a relatively short time the Wampanoags and the Narragansetts had been exterminated. Chief Metacom was hunted down and killed in 1676, and his head was cut off and displayed at Plymouth for twenty years. In addition, Metacom's wife and son were captured and sold into slavery.

Acoma Pueblo in New Mexico, one of several sites at which the Pueblos revolted against the Spanish invaders. (Elaine S. Querry)

For two hundred years such events were repeated time after time as the European intruders pushed further and further inland.

It's important to remember that Christopher Columbus did not step from his ship and into an empty wilderness — a New World ready for colonization — as has so long been taught. While historians' calculations differ, it is estimated that the number of native peoples occupying the New World at the time of Columbus' First Voyage was between 40 and 120 million people and that an estimated fifteen million of those natives were living on the North American continent north of Mexico — that is, in what is today the United States and Canada. Two hundred years after contact — in 1692 — the population of native people in all of North America, including Mexico and Central America, has been estimated at possibly no more than four million. In 1792, there were perhaps a million natives north of Mexico, and half that number in 1892.

Today there are nearly two million native people in the United States alone.

4 Indian Wars

Extermination is the ultimate act of discrimination. In view of the fact that our concern in this chapter is with how discrimination was manifested in this country's wars between whites and Indians, we would do well to begin by considering the very words by which these wars have been, and continue to be to this day, characterized in history books. It is perhaps most revealing that when a battle of any importance is described in our history books, the Indians who engage in the fighting are most often referred to as either "hostiles" or "friendlies," depending, of course, on which side they are fighting. It is revealing, too, that in those instances where the Indians were victorious, the battle is usually referred to as a "massacre."

The traditional American ideal of "patriotism" — that is, a people's right and obligation to defend home and country, to give up one's life for a just cause, to stand up for freedom and religion, and not to allow anyone to take away that right and obligation — seems never to have been extended to those native people who sought to defend their homes and to turn back those who invaded their land. History books term Indians who sought to drive the intruders away and defend themselves and their families not patriots but rather "hostiles." On the other hand, those who meekly accepted the white man's rule and religion are described as "civilized" or "friendly."

Conquest by Violence

Up to this point we have seen that it was the practice of the European invaders — the white settlers — from the earliest colonial days, to utilize the violence of war as their principle method of acquiring additional land and enslaving the native people that were already occupying that land. Even though they considered themselves to be, for the most part, the most pious of people, the colonists considered the Indians who were their neighbors to be brute savages — less than human creatures that had no souls and so were subject to enslavement at best and extermination at worst.

We have seen how the English colonists at Jamestown, Virginia, carried out a bitter war against the Powhatan Confederacy and how they burned villages to the ground, destroyed crops, and ultimately how they served poisoned wine to the Indians even as they sat together during treaty talks. We know, too, that the Powhatan people were reported by the British to have been entirely wiped out as a result of their refusal to give up lands to the colonists.

The conflicts that occurred between Indians and whites during the Colonial period were not always recorded. And those that were recorded were often done so inaccurately. Still, we do know that besides the Powhatan conflict and the King Phillip War of the Wampanoag and Narragansett Tribes in 1675-1677 discussed earlier, there took place in 1637 the Pequot War, which resulted in the virtual extermination of the Pequot society and the clearing of that peoples' Connecticut Valley for further settlement by the whites.

Certainly New England and the colonies weren't the only places where Native Americans fought to hold on to their lands. Spaniards had moved north from Mexico into what is now Arizona and New Mexico as early as 1540. There the Conquistadores and the priests that accompanied them had conquered more than one hundred Indian *pueblos*, or villages. Under Spanish domination, as they had been under British, the native people were forced into slavery and their lands were taken from them. In the Southwest, too, the Indians were denied the practice of their long established religious beliefs. The Spanish were brutally unrelenting in their zeal to convert the natives to

In 1862, thirty-eight Sioux leaders were hanged at Mankato, Minnesota. (Library of Congress)

Catholicism. Finally, led by an Indian named Popé from San Juan Pueblo in New Mexico, the Indians rose up in revolt in 1680. They drove the Spaniards from Santa Fe and other settlements back into Mexico and in so doing regained control of their homeland. For the next dozen years Popé and his people lived in relative peace until, after a bloody battle at Santa Fe in 1693, the Spanish colony was reestablished among the Pueblos along the upper Rio Grande. Meanwhile, in the Southeast yet another native society was being exterminated. As the result of disputes between tribal leaders and traders in South Carolina, the Westo Tribe was wiped out in 1680. In 1711 colonists in North Carolina fought the Tuscarora War, and the Creek Tribe joined forces with the Yamasees in 1715 to engage Carolinian colonists for twelve years in the Yamasee War.

In 1762 an Ottawa chief by the name of Pontiac organized a great confederacy of tribes to fight against the British who had invaded the Ohio River Valley in the Middle West. In 1763 Pontiac and his forces captured no fewer than ten British forts in the region, attacked Fort Detroit and Fort Pitt, and raided settlements in Virginia and Pennsylvania. In 1774 tribes of the southern Ohio River Valley — Delaware, Wyandot, Cayuga Iroquois, and Shawnee — were defeated in what is called Lord Dunsmore's War in West Virginia, and, as a result, the Indians lost forever their hunting grounds south of the Ohio River.

The records of the Bureau of Indian Affairs for the period are spotty and incomplete, to be sure, but they indicate that there were some sixty-five wars between 1782, when there was an attack by Indians on a settlement in Pennsylvania, and 1890, the year of the terrible massacre at Wounded Knee in South Dakota.

In 1862 the Santee Sioux, angered by the fact that the government had reneged on treaty promises, attacked and destroyed nearly every farm and white settlement in southern Minnesota. On December 23 of that year one of the largest mass executions in U.S. history occurred when thirty-eight Sioux leaders were hanged at Mankato, Minnesota. And it is important to note that the execution took place at the order of President Abraham Lincoln.

And still there was trouble in the Southwest. The Navajos of Arizona and New Mexico were a constant irritant to the U.S. government due to their frequent raids against white settlers, Mexicans, and other Indians in the region. In 1863 Kit Carson was dispatched with a force of seven hundred men into Navajoland to put an end, once and for all to "the Navajo problem." Carson and his troops burned crops, slaughtered sheep, and cut down peach trees. The Navajos were expected to either surrender or to starve. In 1864, Carson invaded and attacked the Navajo's Canyon de Chelly in northeast Arizona and took twenty-four hundred Indians who survived on the "Long Walk" to the Bosque Redondo internment camp at Fort Sumner, New Mexico. Eventually eighty-five hundred Navajos were imprisoned at Fort Sumner, an extremely inhospitable place, until 1868, when the government set aside three and a half million acres of arid land in New Mexico and Arizona for the Navajo Reservation.

The Sand Creek Massacre

One of the most horrible massacres of the so-called Indian Wars took place in 1864. In what has been described as "a few hours of madness," a force of more than seven hundred Colorado Volunteers under the command of former Methodist preacher Colonel John M. Chivington attacked and slaughtered a peaceful village of Cheyenne and Arapaho families at Sand Creek, Colorado, killing 133 men, women, and children, and then mutilating their bodies unspeakably.

Chivington was clearly one of the most blatantly racist officers ever to command troops against the Indians. Known to have previously ordered his men to "kill all Indians you come across," Chivington had once made a public speech in Denver advocating the killing and scalping of all Indians, even infants.

There were reportedly six hundred Cheyenne and Arapaho Indians camped at Sand Creek in November of 1864, fully four hundred of whom were women and children. At the center of the Cheyenne camp was the tepee of *Motavato* (Black Kettle), who had been told by the Commissioner of Indian Affairs that as long as the flag of the United States flew above him, no soldier would fire at him or his people. Black Kettle gathered hundreds of Cheyenne women and children around him and his flag, telling them not to be afraid, that the troops would not shoot at them. It was then that Chivington's mob opened fire.

The Sand Creek Massacre. (Colorado Historical Society)

Another Cheyenne leader, seventy-five-year-old White Antelope is said to have walked toward the troops and called out to them, in English, to "Stop!" Then he is reported to have stood with his arms folded until he was shot down.

The Arapaho Left Hand was just then trying to lead his people to the safety of Black Kettle's flag. Left Hand is reported also to have stood with his arms folded across his chest, telling his people that the white men were his friends and would not harm them. Like the others, Left Hand was shot down.

From Congressional Documents we can read firsthand accounts of some of the atrocities that were carried out against the Indians that day at Sand Creek: "Every one I saw dead was scalped. I saw one squaw cut open with an unborn child. . . . I saw the body of White Antelope with the privates cut off. . . . I saw a number of infants in arms killed with their mothers. . . ."

And: "I did not see the body of a man, woman, or child but was scalped, and in many instances their bodies were mutilated in the most horrible manner. . . ."

Surely those few hours of madness at Sand Creek were among the darkest in the history of this country's treatment of its native people.

_____

Wounded Knee

The Sand Creek Massacre of 1864 marked the beginning of the final, best known, period of Indian warfare. The end of that final period was marked by the event at Wounded Knee, South Dakota, in December of 1890 in what was yet another massacre of Native Americans by heavily armed government troops. During the quarter of a century that passed between those two events, there were recorded several other violent clashes between Indians and whites.

In April of 1871 a force of 148 men — white, Mexican, and Papago Indian — attacked an Indian village at Camp Grant north of Tucson. In a matter of minutes, the attackers killed upwards of one hundred Indians, mostly women and children. Only eight Indian men were counted among the dead at Camp Grant that day — the warriors of the village were said to be away hunting at the time. In addition to those killed, twenty-eight children were taken captive.

While the Apaches in the Southwest continued to fight until 1900, the most significant events of the Apache wars ended with the surrender of Geronimo and his band in 1886.

The story of the defeat of Custer at the Little Big Horn is well documented, and we saw in Chapter 2 how Sitting Bull was killed while resisting arrest by Indian policemen. With the death of Sitting Bull, Big Foot took command of the Sioux — 120 men and 230 women and children — and, though he was coughing blood (so sick was he with pneumonia), led his people toward Pine Ridge where he hoped that the last of the great Sioux chiefs,

Red Cloud, could protect them from the soldiers. Before the Sioux reached Pine Ridge however, they were intercepted on December 28th by troops of the infamous Seventh Cavalry and ordered to go to a cavalry camp at Wounded Knee Creek.

Early on the morning of December 29, the troopers gathered up all the weapons from Big Foot's people. When a young Sioux warrior waved a rifle above his head in defiance, the soldiers opened fire on the Indians. It has been estimated that within a matter of minutes fully three hundred of the original three hundred and fifty men, women, and children lay dead or dying on the frozen grass at Wounded Knee. The soldiers lost twenty-

Some of the Major Sites in the Indian Wars

five dead and thirty-nine wounded — most of these the victims of their own rifle- and cannonfire. Years later the massacre at Wounded Knee was termed "most reprehensible, most unjustifiable, and worthy of the severest condemnation" by the very general who had dispatched the soldiers in the first place. And yet for all of this, Custer's old regiment received no fewer than twenty Congressional Medals of Honor.

5 Removal

The massacre at Wounded Knee is considered by many to mark the final chapter in the carnage that was the Indian wars. Yet while the overt killing of Native Americans may have ended, for the most part, as official government policy at the turn of the century (and there can be little doubt it was policy: on July 7, 1876 *The New York Times* reported that some officials in the War Department were seeking *"a policy of extermination of the Indians . . . the speedier the better"*), the policies that followed were just as insidious and, in many cases, equally devastating.

While it's true that war may well have been the most immediate and certainly the most bloody of this country's policies toward its native people, it was clearly not the only method by which the United States sought to deal with the so-called "Indian problem."

History books have long explained this country's growth and development in terms of brave and honorable men engaging in heroic exploration and expansion. The textbook story of America has been, as one historian has described it, one of "glorious military conquest, of wresting virgin country from savages, of subduing and taming the Wild." If the plight of the native people has been dealt with at all in these accounts, it has generally been in terms of painted bands of heathen redskins making generally unprovoked sneak attacks upon the wagon trains of an advancing civilization of brave white men.

Besides extermination, the history of the United States' response to the very presence of a native population in areas where settlement and commerce was desired, has been marked

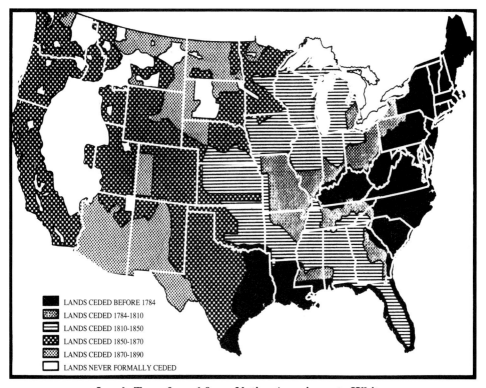

LANDS CEDED BEFORE 1784
LANDS CEDED 1784-1810
LANDS CEDED 1810-1850
LANDS CEDED 1850-1870
LANDS CEDED 1870-1890
LANDS NEVER FORMALLY CEDED

Lands Transferred from Native Americans to Whites

Credit: Redrawn from *Atlas of the North American Indian*, 6.6

by a policy of *removal*. That is, if the native people could not for whatever reason be exterminated, then they were to be moved elsewhere — to some distant place where they would no longer be a bother. It simply cannot be too strongly emphasized here that the "Indian problem" in America was — and, some would maintain, *is* — a problem of Indian people occupying land that the larger white society desired for its own use.

We know today that removal as a solution to this perceived "Indian problem" had been going on in a more or less haphazard way since the early Colonial period. As European settlers determined that they required more land, they pushed the Indian people further west — into the interior of the country — onto land that the intruders did not consider habitable or valuable in any way. Sometimes this removal was forced upon the Indians by war *and* sometimes it was accomplished by agreement, that is, by treaty between the white government and the Indian people. And sometimes removal was accomplished through a combination of war *and* treaty. We have seen examples of how it was when removal was forced by bullets and cannons, we will now consider the policy of removal by treaty.

Andrew Jackson and the Indian Removal Act

Removal was effectively established as a national policy with the election of Andrew Jackson to the presidency of the United States in 1828. Jackson had grown up in a time of hostility to the Indian; moreover, he had commanded troops during the Indian wars. As president he believed that tribes should be removed west of the Mississippi, to areas where the advancing white settlements would not be disturbed by the Indians' activities. Furthermore, Jackson favored *immediate* removal *by any means* — including force if necessary. And while it's true Jackson's policy would give individual Indians the choice of conforming to the white man's ways and remaining in the vicinity of his homeland, or of removing west with his tribe immediately

INDIAN LAND FOR SALE

GET A HOME
OF
YOUR OWN
❋
EASY PAYMENTS

PERFECT TITLE
❋
POSSESSION
WITHIN
THIRTY DAYS

FINE LANDS IN THE WEST

IRRIGATED
IRRIGABLE

GRAZING

AGRICULTURAL
DRY FARMING

IN 1910 THE DEPARTMENT OF THE INTERIOR SOLD UNDER SEALED BIDS ALLOTTED INDIAN LAND AS FOLLOWS:

Location.	Acres.	Average Price per Acre.	Location.	Acres.	Average Price per Acre.
Colorado	5,211.21	$7.27	Oklahoma	34,664.00	$19.14
Idaho	17,013.00	24.85	Oregon	1,020.00	15.43
Kansas	1,684.50	33.45	South Dakota	120,445.00	16.53
Montana	11,034.00	9.86	Washington	4,879.00	41.37
Nebraska	5,641.00	36.65	Wisconsin	1,069.00	17.00
North Dakota	22,610.70	9.93	Wyoming	865.00	20.64

FOR THE YEAR 1911 IT IS ESTIMATED THAT **350,000** ACRES WILL BE OFFERED FOR SALE

For information as to the character of the land write for booklet, "INDIAN LANDS FOR SALE," to the Superintendent U. S. Indian School at any one of the following places:

CALIFORNIA: Hoopa.	**MINNESOTA:** Onigum.	**NORTH DAKOTA:** Fort Totten. Fort Yates.	**OKLAHOMA—Con.** Sac and Fox Agency. Shawnee. Wyandotte.	**SOUTH DAKOTA:** Cheyenne Agency. Crow Creek. Greenwood.	**WASHINGTON:** Fort Simcoe. Fort Spokane. Tekoa.
COLORADO: Ignacio.	**MONTANA:** Crow Agency.	**OKLAHOMA:** Anadarko.	**OREGON:** Klamath Agency.	Lower Brule. Pine Ridge.	Tulalip.
IDAHO: Lapwai.	**NEBRASKA:** Macy.	Cantonment. Colony.	Pendleton. Roseburg.	Rosebud. Sisseton.	**WISCONSIN:** Oneida.
KANSAS: Horton. Nadeau.	Santee. Winnebago.	Darlington. Muskogee, SUPT. OF UNION AGENT. Pawnee.	Siletz.		

WALTER L. FISHER,
Secretary of the Interior.

ROBERT G. VALENTINE,
Commissioner of Indian Affairs.

The policy of removal was an excuse for grabbing Indian lands that had not already been taken by force. (Library of Congress)

and doing as he pleased, it is clear that such a "solution" was short-sighted. Certainly it should have been obvious that it was only a matter of time before the white settlers would cast greedy eyes upon the lands to the west. As president however, Jackson placed the emphasis of his Indian policy on a solution that was politically expedient rather than one which was permanent. In 1830 Congress passed the Indian Removal Act in support of Jackson's position.

Removal in Action: The Case of the Choctaw

While we must keep in mind the fact that removal as a policy was implemented in general among the various tribes, we can focus on a single tribe's experience as an example of the results of that policy.

The aboriginal Choctaw people were living peacefully in what is today the state of Mississippi when their first contact with Europeans occurred in 1540. It was in that year that the Spanish explorer Hernando de Soto invaded their homeland and massacred some 1,500 tribespeople. Nearly three hundred years later, when President Jackson's Indian Removal Act was passed into law, it was the Choctaw Tribe that would be the first to make the long trek west from Mississippi to Indian Territory (Oklahoma). The removal of the Choctaw was significant not only because it established the pattern for Indian removal in the United States, but also because it ultimately influenced the existence of almost every Indian nation in the country.

In 1830 the Choctaw Nation, by the terms of the Treaty of Dancing Rabbit Creek, ceded to the United States all of their homeland east of the Mississippi River in exchange for land in Indian Territory in what is now Oklahoma. The choice of the Choctaw by the War Department to inaugurate the implementation of the new policy of removal was made primarily on account of the tribe's long history of friendly cooperation with the U.S. government. At the time the tribe numbered between

18,000 and 20,000, and removal was scheduled to be carried out in three stages: the first in 1831, followed by removals in 1832 and 1833.

According to Article 14 of the Treaty of Dancing Rabbit Creek, those tribal members who elected to stay in Mississippi and "conform to the white man's way" were required to register with the Indian Agent within a period of six months. Once registered, those Choctaw who remained were to be allotted parcels of land as reservations. The Indian agent at the time was William Ward, who, because he wanted all of the Indians removed from the state, was strongly opposed to Article 14 of the treaty and delayed registering the Choctaw as long as possible. (It was reported that Ward sometimes pretended to be ill and even went into hiding in order to deny the Indians their treaty rights.) While approximately six thousand Choctaw eventually elected to remain in Mississippi, only sixty-nine heads of Choctaw families were ever officially registered by Ward, thereby assuring that the vast majority were never to receive the allotments of land to which they were entitled.

In the late fall of 1831 the first group of Choctaw began their long, sad walk. And it must be stressed that the removal to Indian Territory was to be, in fact, a *walk* — for as stipulated in the "Removal Regulations": ". . . all of the Indians would remove on foot except the young and infirm." Unusually severe weather and widespread disease among the people, combined with short supplies and meager rations to make for terrible suffering and incredible hardships for the Indians that winter.

The migrations of the following two years were similarly disastrous. While the weather was not so severe as it had been during the winter of 1831, the government had cut back drastically on the funds allocated for the removal and, as a result, food and shelter were in even shorter supply.

When the last large group of Choctaw arrived in Indian Territory in the spring of 1834, it brought the total Choctaw population there to about 11,500. Approximately 14,000 Indians had departed Mississippi on the three removal walks; more than 2,500 had died during their hard journey west.

A traditional Indian dwelling with Washington Monument in the background; an ironic commentary on the U.S. government's repeated failures to deal honorably with Native Americans. (John Neubauer)

The history of the United States' treaty policies toward Native American people is one of shameful expediency, at best. Treaties were made with Indians time and again, only to be broken by the government at the first sign that the stipulations of a particular treaty were no longer most favorable to non-Indian interests. When white settlers moving west pressed for opening up new lands, treaties were ignored, or at best rewritten to suit the new demands — never mind that the Indians proved to be the losers without exception.

6 Assimilation

Up to this point we've examined the ways in which Native Americans have suffered discrimination in terms of attempts at their extermination by the military; through their negotiation of treaties with an all too often dishonest and unreliable white government; and by means of their removal and relocation in a federally approved policy wherein whole tribes were pushed westward and concentrated onto generally worthless and ever-shrinking lands termed "reservations." In this chapter we will look at the federal policy that came to be known as *assimilation*.

The Philosophy of Assimilation

Assimilation has been variously defined. According to the Commission on the Rights, Liberties, and Responsibilities of the American Indian (1966), the Bureau of Indian Affairs in 1905 considered an Indian assimilated if he wore "civilian dress." In 1947 an assistant commissioner of Indian Affairs defined assimilation in terms of how much white blood the Indian had, his literacy, business ability, acceptance of non-Indian institutions, and his acceptance by whites. In their Report of 1966, the Commission maintains that "no tests yet devised show whether an individual Indian has changed his basic emotions," and concludes that "regardless of the degree of acculturation . . . a persistent core of aboriginal goals and expectations is still discernible in some Indians."

Members of the Friends of the Indian Reform movement — reportedly earnest men and women who considered themselves

Sioux boys upon arrival at the Indian Trade School at Carlisle, Pennsylvania. (National Archives)

to be the true friends of native people—sought to eliminate altogether the "Indian Problem" by working to see to it that there simply would no longer exist any people identifiable as Indians. It was these reformers—many of whom were Indian agents and missionaries—who were largely responsible for the policy of assimilation.

It must be made clear at the outset that patriotism and religion were the guiding principals of these reformers, and, convinced that their cause was right and just (and that God most certainly approved), they saw no reason to try and discover anything positive in the Indians' way of life—certainly they never inquired as to the Indians' wishes in the matter. Rather they decided that the Indian should become a good American—that it was the Christian duty of right-thinking white reformers to destroy all aspects of native life so that there might remain no way of distinguishing the American Indian from anyone else. The aim of these reformers then, was the complete assimilation of native people into the mainstream of white culture.

As a Commissioner of Indian Affairs of the time put it, the goal was to *make the Indians feel at home in America*. Certainly it is ironic that the American Indian has traditionally been viewed as "other" in this country—that is, viewed as somehow different from "typical" Americans. The white reformers, these members of the Friends of the Indians movement, considered themselves to be the best possible models of what a good American should be and so naturally sought to erase all differences that distinguished the native people from themselves—differences in dress, language, culture, and religious beliefs. The reformers sought to accomplish this in basically three ways: first, to eradicate the Indians' tribal relations and their reservation base and to individualize the Indian on small homesteads by means of the allotment of land in severalty; then they sought to grant these land-holding Indians full American citizenship along with the protection and restraints of the law that comes along with that citizenship; and third, to provide a government-run school system that would properly educate the younger Indians in order to mold them into the patriotic and Christian Americans that they should become.

════════════════════

The Severalty Act

Not surprisingly, the allotment of land in severalty was to prove a two-edged sword. That is to say, while on the surface it appeared that the native people were to benefit from gaining individual title to land, in fact non-Indian citizens stood to gain as much or often more. It must be pointed out that the reformers were of the strong belief that civilization could come about—that is, Indians would become *civilized*—only when private ownership of a plot of land instilled in the owner of that land the incentive to work hard. In the simplest terms, then, it was thought that in order to be a good American, one was supposed to own property and work hard—this was the "American way." Never mind that the Native American did not consider the land around him to be something that one could "own"—after all, the land was there for everyone to live upon and, just as important, to live in concert with. The idea of private ownership of land was totally alien to native people. Indian tribes traditionally lived communally—it was the "Indian way."

Along with the allotment of land came citizenship and its system of laws. Again, never mind that the government of the United States had solemnly and repeatedly promised the Indians that they would never lose the use of their tribal lands nor be subjected to the laws of the white population—unless, that is, they were first consulted and had agreed. We may recall that, according to the 1830 Treaty of Dancing Rabbit Creek, one such promise was that "no state or territory shall ever have a right to pass laws for the government of the Choctaw nation of red people and their descendents: and that no part of the land granted them shall ever be embraced in any territory or state."

The other side of the allotment issue—the other edge of the sword, as it were—was that the "surplus" lands left after the

Tesuque children learning numbers in their own language; today, many Indian schools seek to preserve their traditions. (Mary Kate Denny/PhotoEdit)

allotments on a reservation had been made were to be open to white settlement. If we take the number of tribal members and multiply that total by the acres of land to be allotted to each Indian, we see that the result was most often far and away only a fraction of the total reservation land. If, for example, there were 500,000 acres on a reservation of 1,000 Indians and each was allotted 150 acres, there would remain 350,000 acres that would then be open to white settlement. We know that much of the land promised to the Indians was, after allotment, occupied by white settlers.

Americanization by Force

Believing that neither owning property nor attaining citizenship would do the Indian much good if he didn't have the proper education to appreciate and manage the responsibilities that came along with being a citizen farmer, the reformers focused their concerns on education. The Friends of the Indian, in concert with the Bureau of Indian Affairs, strove for nothing less than the total Americanization of the native people through education. The primary goal, of course, was to destroy *Indianness*, to do away completely with tribalism.

The way to accomplish Americanization, the reformers believed, was through education. And if the Indians were unwilling to accept their Americanization voluntarily, it would be forced upon them.

Clearly, one aim of the reform movement was to assure that Indians would no longer be concentrated on reservations where they would not have the benefit of close proximity to good role models — that is, contact with *white* citizens. Again, failing to discover a single positive aspect of native culture, these friends of the Indian were determined to see to it that the Indians abandon completely their savage culture, their native language, and their heathen religious practices. Before the red man could be civilized — before he could become an American — he first would have to learn to think, act, speak, and live like an American.

Ultimately then, the goal of the reformers was to assimilate the native population completely into white American society. Private ownership of property, education, citizenship and adherence to law, and the acceptance of the white ideal of Christian moral principles were all means to that end: the end being transformation of the Native American into neat replicas of the white reformers. In fact, however, the assimilation movement was a disaster—for the Indians and for the United States.

The concept of forcing plots of land on individuals whose whole existence had always been tied to strong communal traditions turned out to be a failure: title to a small farm did not result in the sudden transformation of Indians into white farmers.

Forced schooling rarely produced the patriotic Christian citizens that were the goal of the schoolmasters; rather, it resulted in the tragic loss of the Indians' cultural identity and did more than anything else to demoralize a once proud people. Little wonder, considering what we find when we examine the attitudes of some of those schoolmasters.

Richard H. Pratt, for example, was the founder and for twenty-five years the superintendent of the Indian Trade School at Carlisle, Pennsylvania—one of the widely respected schools of its kind. Yet listen to these words which Pratt spoke in an address to a Denver conference of Charities and Correction in 1892:

"A great general has said that the only good Indian is a dead one, and that high sanction of his destruction has been an enormous factor in promoting Indian massacres. In a sense, I agree with the sentiment, but only in this: that all the Indian there is in the race should be dead. Kill the Indian in him, and save the man."

Clearly, Pratt's attitudes toward Indian students were based on arrogant, racist assumptions of white superiority—the same kind of assumptions that allowed many white people to look down on blacks. It is revealing that Pratt believed, and more telling still that he made public the belief, that slavery was not without its benefits for the slaves:

"Horrible as were the experiences of its introduction, and of slavery itself, there was concealed in them the greatest blessing

A Hopi Kachina; whites who enforced assimilation were blind to the vibrant diversity of Native American cultures. (David Young-Wolff/PhotoEdit)

that ever came to the Negro race — seven millions of blacks from cannibalism in darkest Africa to citizenship in free and enlightened America. . . . Left in Africa, surrounded by their fellow-savages, our seven millions of industrious black fellow-citizens would still be savages."

The Friends of the Indian Reform Movement had operated under the self-righteous belief that their cause — a cause that was aimed at engulfing and swallowing up completely the Indian — was righteous and correct. In truth, it was a disaster.

7 The Indian on Film

Before there were films, there were books; but while the American Indian has always been a popular subject of American popular literature, our focus here will be on the portrayal of native people on film.

Movie Stereotypes

In Chapter 1 we touched briefly upon the notion that scholars whose job is to study how it is we come to hold the attitudes that we do have long believed that audiences of motion pictures (and, we may assume, television) tend to believe that the images of events and people that they are seeing on the screen are true. This is especially the case in those instances when the events and people portrayed are unknown or foreign to the viewer. For example, audiences who watched early Tarzan movies — that is, those who had no previous experience with Africa or Africans — came to believe that spear-carrying native African people walked around with bones in their noses and addressed dashing white hunters as "Um-gaw-wa B'wana." Closer to home, early moviegoers who lived in segregated communities saw American blacks portrayed (when portrayed at all) as comical, bug-eyed clowns — lazy buffoons who spent their days singing and dancing.

What is particularly important with respect to an unquestioning belief in what we see portrayed on the screen, is the fact that *realism* has never been a necessarily important factor in American motion pictures. Movies, after all, have traditionally been made primarily to earn money for moviemakers by appealing to large audiences. This has been especially true in the case of Hollywood's portrayal of the American Indian.

If we think about it, we can see that there is the danger that we might rely on movies for too much of our knowledge of the world outside of our own time and beyond our own community. Some social critics have argued that motion pictures have, as much as anything, been *responsible* for the stereotype image of the American Indian, while others have maintained that, in truth, Hollywood merely *reflects* (projects) onto the screen the values and attitudes held by the majority of American society. The argument is perhaps a little like the debate over which came first, the chicken or the egg. The fact that Indians have rarely been portrayed with any degree of accuracy on the screen certainly reflects the way the larger (white) society has viewed them, but these distorted film portrayals of native people have not merely reflected existing attitudes — they have also validated and reinforced such stereotypes.

Commercial popular entertainment — that is, entertainment that seeks to appeal to the broadest possible audience in order to gain the profits that come with success — depends for its appeal on the use of familiar stories and stereotyped characters portrayed by well-known performers. We know that audiences who watch movies have come to expect certain things to occur (familiar stories) and to expect characters to appear and act in a generally predictable manner (stereotyped characters). In the case of Native Americans, the expectations have most often been based upon misconceptions in the first place. For example the feathered headdresses, skillful horsemanship, reliance on hunting, the buckskin clothing — all the things that we have come to expect of the typical Indian in motion pictures — were characteristic of only about two dozen Plains Indian tribes in the 1800s. And certainly movie Indians have rarely been portrayed by Hollywood as speaking in anything other than the grunting pidgin-English of the rude, uneducated savage. If Hollywood has reinforced the popular misconceptions about Indians—and there is ample evidence to support the notion that it has—we should remember that these misconceptions were not new when the first motion pictures appeared.

Early Depictions of Indians on Film

The first films to show Indians as the primary subject matter were among the first movies ever made. Short documentaries of less than a minute in length, they were filmed in the 1890s and contained scenes of Indians dancing and, interestingly enough, receiving their rations from their white benefactors.

The narrative form—that is, the dramatic story rather than the documentary—was early on to become the accepted form for motion pictures. One of the first narrative films was a 1903 production titled *Kit Carson* that showed the famous scout and a group of innocent trappers being attacked and murdered by savage Indians. The trappers are all murdered, that is. Kit Carson himself survives when an "Indian maiden" helps him escape, a deed for which she is later killed by the savage Indian chief. In a film produced the following year, Kit Carson and his friends strike back with a sound (and deadly) defeat of a band of vicious Indians who have savagely massacred a white pioneer family.

Even the early ads for movies contributed to the vicious Indian stereotype: A press release in 1911 called the film *Ogallalah*, "Savage and cruel—as Indians are by nature." The idea, then, of savage redskins attacking innocent white settlers had begun to be portrayed as entertainment as early as 1903. The brutal slaughter of women and children by the red heathens seems first to have shown up on the screen in 1913 in *The Battle of Elderbush Gulch*. One advertising poster for this movie shows a fearsomely scowling Indian—we know he's an Indian because he's wearing feathers in his hair and a breechcloth—kneeling over what is clearly a white woman. And, as if that's not terrible enough, the savage redskin is about to hurl a wild-eyed, blond-haired child down upon the lifeless body of its mother.

Early motion pictures also helped to establish the stereotype of the beautiful Indian princess or maiden ("squaws" were generally old and fat) who, like the legendary Pocahontas, would come to the aid of the good whites even though to do so meant denying her own race and tribe. In the 1908 film, *The Kentuckian*, for example, an Indian maiden rescues a handsome young white man, marries him, gives birth to his son, and then kills herself so that he can return to white society without embarrassment. In a 1913 film titled *The Squaw Man*, an Indian woman commits suicide in order to prevent fighting between whites and Indians and so that her white husband might send their half-breed son off to school. (*The Squaw Man* was so successful that it was remade in 1918 and again in 1931.) The device of the Indian wife who dies continued for many years: *A Man Called Horse* (1970), *Little Big Man* (1971), *Jeremiah Johnson* (1972), *The Man Who Loved Cat Dancing* (1973) — all included white men married to Indian women who die as a part of the plot.

Early motion pictures evidenced strong prejudice against the Indian with the notion that it was somehow beyond his nature to improve himself in ways acceptable to white society. The Indian was a savage beast, and that, according to the prejudice, was simply that. An advertisement for the 1908 film, *Call of the Wild*, reads: "So it is with the Redman. Civilization cannot bleach his tawny epidermis, and that will always prove an insurmountable barrier to social distinction."

In the movie, an Indian honor student and football hero at the Carlisle Indian School falls in love with a white girl who is shocked by his attentions and rejects him. The Indian, unable to maintain his civilized state in the face of his heartache, reverts to his heathen ways by dressing up like a savage in buckskin and feathers and carrying off the girl against her will.

Stereotypes Reinforced

The late 1930s and 1940s saw a continuation of the stereotypical portrayals of Indians in films that ignored historical

Images of the Indian on film rarely reflect the everyday reality of Indian life. (Richard Hutchings/InfoEdit)

accuracy in favor of American patriotism. For example, Custer's Last Stand was dramatically and inaccurately portrayed at least eight times during this period. Without exception, Custer was pictured as a hero — a patriotic American who died a martyr to the cause of manifest destiny.

The 1940 epic *Northwest Passage* is probably the most violently anti-Indian movie ever made about the conquest of the frontier. In this film, Major Rogers (played by Spencer Tracy) leads his men into an Indian village and there delivers a hysterical speech about the horrors of Indian atrocities. He then orders his men to kill every Indian man, woman, and child. As the film ends we see the major silhouetted against the sky, his slaughter of the Indians, according to some critics, apparently having made him into a kind of frontier saint.

Other, more recent movies perpetuate the racism that was at the heart of the Indian wars. In *The Searchers* (1956), John Wayne plays a man driven by a burning hatred of Indians. At the end of the film we learn that civilization is preserved only when whites attack a sleeping village of Comanche and slaughter nearly everyone — including the women and children.

In the 1964 film, *Cheyenne Autumn*, a troop of United States Cavalry harasses a small band of Indians whose only desire is to escape internment in Oklahoma and return to their Yellowstone homeland. Also remarkable is the fact that the five principle Indian characters of *Cheyenne Autumn* were all played by non-Indian actors.

When motion pictures (and later television) portrayed "good" Indians, it was generally as faithful Indian companions to the noble white man. The Lone Ranger, with his Indian sidekick Tonto, was originally created for radio in 1932. In 1938 the show was translated to the motion picture screen, and from 1949 until 1960 the Masked Man and his Indian Friend were featured in a television series. There was a 1981 movie in which Tonto seems to have experienced a slightly raised consciousness, but he remained even then little more than a sidekick to his *Kemo Sabe*.

Notable Exceptions

There have been attempts to show the "Indian side" of history, to be sure. Most notable among them are *Soldier Blue* (1970), which was based partly on the tragic Sand Creek Massacre in Colorado, and included graphic scenes of brutal white men slaughtering Indian women and children. More popular is *Little Big Man* (1971), in which Custer is portrayed as a mad man. (Interestingly, in the film, Little Big Man is the Indian name of Jack Crabb, a white man who was captured as a child and lives much of his life as an Indian.) And in *Ulzana's Raid* (1972) we see that while the Indians' savagery is consistent with their cultural beliefs, the equally savage actions of the whites are purely the result of racism.

A perhaps lesser known, but interesting film is the long-titled, *Buffalo Bill and the Indians, or Sitting Bull's History Lesson* (1976) wherein the famous Indian fighter and showman is portrayed (by Paul Newman) as a drunken, wig-wearing braggart who reveals at one point that he has a "better sense of history than the truth," while Sitting Bull is shown to be the proud and noble, true man of the West — a man who, unlike the whites, is completely at home on the frontier. The film makes note of many of the injustices suffered by Native Americans. At one point, the Indians remind Buffalo Bill that his people seem always to find it necessary to kill not only the warriors but also "every old man, woman, child, and dog in the village." When President Cleveland visits the Wild West Show, Sitting Bull takes the opportunity to try and ask one thing of the Great White Father. Cleveland not only refuses to hear Sitting Bull's request, but also tells the Indian that the answer would be "no" if he *did* hear the question. Buffalo Bill takes this as a great example of American patriotism and announces that it shows the difference between a president and a chief: a president "knows enough to retaliate *before* it's his turn." While we may like these Indians much better than we do the whites, in the end we learn that Sitting Bull has been killed by the police who came to arrest him, and we watch as Buffalo Bill ritually defeats, in hand-to-hand combat, and then symbolically scalps, the giant Indian Halsey as the white crowd claps and cheers.

There have been thousands of movies featuring Native American characters, yet only a very few of those have attempted to portray Indian life with any degree of cultural accuracy.

8 Tribal Rights and Economics

In 1775, Indian affairs were the responsibility of the Continental Congress. When the Constitution was adopted, the states gave the power of regulating commerce with Indian tribes over to the federal government. The federal office that was set up to administer Indian affairs was established in 1824 as an agency of the War Department. It was not until 1849 that the administration of Indian affairs was moved to the Department of the Interior, where it has remained to this day.

The Bureau of Indian Affairs

From the time of its inception in 1849, the Bureau of Indian Affairs (BIA) has traditionally maintained firm control over the lives and property of Native American peoples living on or near reservations. Very often the BIA has leased mineral, water, and other rights on the reservations to non-Indians, a practice that often led to charges of mismanagement and conflict of interest by these bureaucratic "managers" of the interests of Indians. The fact that the tribes themselves had virtually no voice in the establishment of BIA policies, nor in the administration of those policies, contributed much to the lingering atmosphere of mistrust and suspicion of the United States government on the part of the Indians. And because they had experienced a long history of betrayals through policies which were supposed to grant them legal and social "equality," that mistrust and suspicion on the part of the Indians was not without a basis in fact.

Prior to 1934, federal Indian policy had two principal goals: the acquisition of Indian lands and the assimilation of native people. Up until that time, the BIA had chiefly maintained its control over Indians residing on reservations through its policies of law enforcement, operation of reservation school systems, and the act of providing welfare to the people. In 1934, Congress passed the Indian Reorganization Act in what was supposed to be an attempt to establish a policy of self-government among Indian tribes. We have seen that that policy was largely ignored.

Termination

In 1953 the Eighty-third Congress of the United States adopted House Concurrent Resolution 108 setting forth the policy of terminating "as fast as possible" the special relationship existing between American Indians and the federal government. Resolution 108 was an attempt by the government to extinguish treaty rights and tribal political existence by ending federal support and protection of certain reservation Indians. While a number of tribes voted in favor of the policy of termination, many traditionalists boycotted meetings called to explain the termination legislation on the grounds that Indian tribes were sovereign nations and therefore could not simply be legislated out of existence by Congress. In those cases where termination took place, it was usually done too quickly and without proper preparation. Some of the tribes affected lacked the ability to take control of what had for so long been managed for them, and the policy of termination was soon abandoned.

The Emergence of Indian Activism

The civil rights movement of the 1960s had a profound affect on Native American people. Young Indians who had seen their

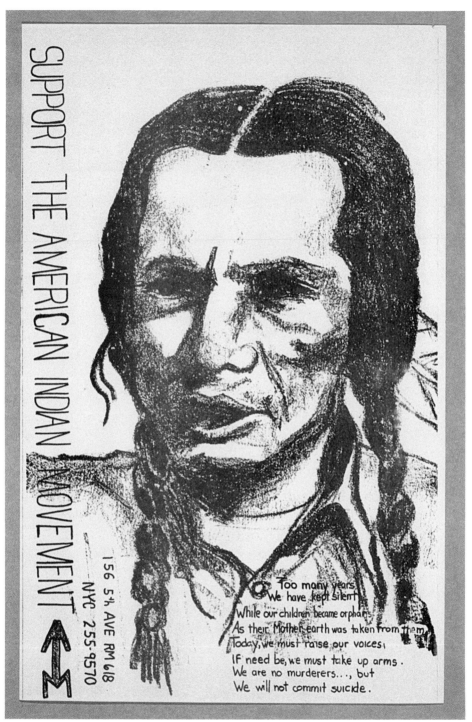

The American Indian Movement is one of the leading Indian rights organizations. (Library of Congress)

parents and grandparents thwarted by the paternalistic bureaucracy of the federal government learned an important lesson from the success of civil rights marches and demonstrations in getting unjust policies changed. It is not surprising, then, that the decade of the sixties saw the emergence of Indian activism.

On November 19, 1969, nearly three hundred activists — under the banner "Indians of All Tribes" — occupied Alcatraz Island, the infamous island in San Francisco Bay that had previously been the site of the legendary federal prison, and demanded that the government give them title to it. In their "Proclamation to the Great White Father and All His People," the occupying Indians reclaimed the island in the tradition of Christopher Columbus: that is, *by right of discovery*." The activists pointed out that Alcatraz was particularly suitable for Indian land because it so clearly fit the white government's standards for an Indian reservation. Alcatraz was, among other things, isolated from modern facilities, it had no running water, inadequate sanitary facilities, there were no health care or educational facilities, and its population had traditionally been held prisoner and kept dependent upon others. The occupation of Alcatraz by the Indians of All Tribes lasted until June, 1971.

In 1972 Indian rights organizations undertook large-scale protest movements aimed at what they saw as injustices carried out against Indian people by the bureaucracy of the BIA. That year members of the American Indian Movement (AIM), under the leadership of Dennis Banks, Clyde Bellecourt, Russell Means, and others — along with various other Indian activist groups — occupied the headquarters of the BIA in Washington, D.C., and demanded strong government action against the discrimination they perceived they were suffering in the areas of jobs and housing. The following year, in 1973, militant members of AIM took control of the village of Wounded Knee, South Dakota, and demanded the return of lands taken from Indians in violation of treaty agreements.

In large part as a result of these confrontations, the Indian Self-Determination and Education Assistance Act was enacted by

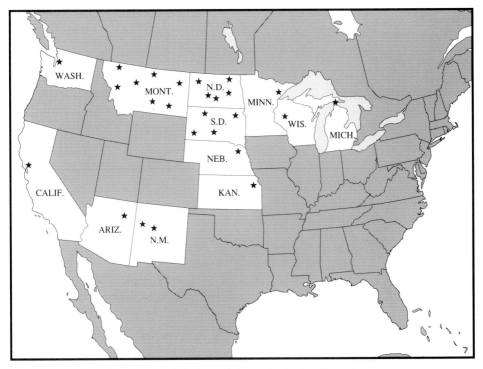

Locations of Indian Colleges in the United States

Congress in 1975. Since that time, many tribes have resumed
control of their schools and law enforcement agencies, as well as
other facilities and activities. Although as recently as 1984 there
were seventy-two Indian day schools operated by the BIA, at the
same time there were sixty-two schools which had been
contracted to Indian groups for their operation. In 1992, in
addition to two predominantly Indian colleges operated by the
BIA, there were twenty-four colleges on or near reservations,
owned and operated by the Indians; all but three of these colleges
were two-year community colleges.

Conditions on the Reservations Today

Are conditions on Indian reservations better to any noticeable
degree than they were, say, fifty years ago? Sad to say, the

answer to that question is that, in many vital areas of life, conditions have not improved.

Today there remains a great disparity between the poor health of Native Americans and the comparative good health of the average citizen of the United States.

Indian health problems are often the result of inadequate sanitary facilities, contaminated water, substandard housing, deficiencies in essential foods, and general ignorance about when and how to obtain what medical services might be available and affordable. And while it is true that the same problems may be said to exist among other impoverished people in the nation, our focus here is upon the Native American segment of the population.

Birth rates among Native Americans are high. In 1980, for example, Indians had the youngest population of all minority groups. The average age of Indians in the United States was twenty-five, compared to the national average of thirty. And among the Navajo — the largest tribe in the United States — the average age of the population was barely seventeen. Young populations are fast-growing populations — the American Indian population grew by 38% during the decade between 1980 and 1990, compared with 6% for Blacks and 13% for non-Hispanic whites. And in New Mexico it has been estimated that American Indians will double their population by the year 2010, and then double it again by 2043!

In 1987 the Western Interstate Commission on Higher Education estimated that by the year 2000, over 50% of the Southwestern population under the age of thirty will be made up of African Americans, American Indians, Asians, and Hispanics. And that by 2080, these four groups will constitute over 50% of the entire U.S. population and their under-thirty population groups will make up 60% to 70% of the nation's total population.

It's important to know that birth-rate figures — especially among Native American populations — are often only estimates and that in many cases births go unreported. For example, a 1960 study conducted on the vast Navajo reservation revealed that 43%

Navajo women in New Mexico shearing sheep. (Paul Conklin/PhotoEdit)

of Navajo births took place outside a hospital and without a doctor in attendance.

While the birth rate among Indians is high, the average life span among the native population is similarly disparate when compared to the rest of the population.

In 1960, the average age at death for reservation Indians was 41.8 years, compared with 62.3 for all races. Moreover, studies reveal Native Americans to be two to eight times more susceptible than non-Indians to many causes of death, including accident, suicide (twice the national average), murder, and cirrhosis of the liver caused by alcohol consumption. (A 1985 study showed that fully three times as many Indians as non-Indians die from alcohol-related causes.) It is especially revealing that when these same studies showed Indians as a group to suffer fewer deaths than the general population from such causes as cancer and heart disease, it was suggested that this difference might simply be due to the fact Indians weren't as likely as the general population to live long enough to suffer the diseases of old age.

Today one need only travel across the vast Navajo country or visit the large and economically troubled Pine Ridge, Rosebud, and Standing Rock reservations in South Dakota or any one of the many other enclaves of Native American people to see that reservation living conditions are, for the most part, squalid and miserable. A 1984 study determined that most rural Indian families were living in shacks, mobile homes, and substandard public housing, and that of the 182,000 native families living on or near reservations at the time, 33,097 were homeless. (The homeless did not include those the study found to be living in tents, tepees, and cars.)

High rates of unemployment can be attributed to the fact that reservations are not generally places of great industry — in many instances jobs are few if they are available at all. For those Indians living in urban areas, we might note that the unemployment rate among Indians in Los Angeles in 1985 was estimated to be 40%; in New York, 45% of the city's Indian community were unemployed; and in Minneapolis-St. Paul, the rate was 49%. At the same time, unemployment rates for all workers in these areas ranged from 4.4% to 8.2%.

Where there is tribal industry, it is often limited to the making and selling of traditional Indian crafts. In addition, there are often valuable natural resources to be found on reservation land. Natural resources here include not only mineral resources such as oil and coal, but also fish and game, the basis for the recreational industry of allowing hunting and fishing for fees on tribal property.

Rights of Sovereignty

Ironically, there is at least one business advantage to being a reservation: *Sovereignty* means the suspension of many local,

A trading post on Route 66 in downtown Gallup, New Mexico. (Elaine S. Querry)

state, and federal laws on Indian territory. Because reservations
have no sales or property taxes, cigarettes, gasoline, and other
items can be sold for low prices. The sale of tax-free cigarettes
has for some years been a popular industry on some reservations
and in some tribal communities. In addition, sovereignty allows
reservations to offer some activities not permitted off-reservation.
Like gambling. Today there are more than one hundred
reservations which allow some form of gaming. By far the most
popular is high-stakes bingo. These gaming operations are
responsible for generating an estimated 400 million dollars a year
in revenue for the various tribes that operate them. With such
impressive amounts of money involved, it is not surprising that
many state governments are now seeking to gain control and tax
the income from the Indian activities that take place on these
federal reservations.

9 Some Who Made a Difference

We have seen that the history of Indian people in the United States is longer than that of any other group. That is to say, we have seen that Native American people — by the very fact that they are *native* or *indigenous* to the region — have occupied the country that we know as the United States far longer than have Anglo-Americans, or African-Americans, or any of the many other hyphenated American groups that make up the population today. We have seen, too, how attitudes of prejudice and the resulting discrimination toward Native Americans have been clearly evidenced from as early as that October day in 1492 when Cristóbal Colón first stepped onto the sand of the Bahamian Island beach and proclaimed his "discovery" of a New World, to as recently as today's newspaper accounts of poverty and alcoholism on reservations. And we have seen how it was that the first European intruders and settlers and later the established government of the United States adopted official policies ranging from enslavement, to extermination, to removal, and finally to termination and assimilation of a whole race of native people as the various "solutions" to what has been viewed as "the Indian problem." While it is important that we highlight a selected number of individuals who have helped to resist or overcome

prejudice and discrimination against Native American people, it
is equally important that we point to and so remember those
individuals — both Indian and non-Indian and in *negative* as well
as in positive terms — who have become symbolic of the kinds of
prejudice and discrimination that are the subject of this study.

Cristóbal Colón (Christopher Columbus, 1451-1506)

First of many to claim the ancestral homeland of Native
American people "by right of discovery," Colón reported that he
believed the natives would make good slaves.

Red Cloud (c.1822-1909)

Red Cloud (*Makhpiya-Luta*) was an Oglala Sioux who had
gained great prestige through feats of bravery as a warrior. As a
young man, Red Cloud had killed Bull Bear, the most powerful
Oglala chief, as the result of a long-standing feud between Bull
Bear and Smoke, Red Cloud's uncle. Never a chief among his
own people, Red Cloud was looked upon (mistakenly) as a top
Sioux chieftain by the white authorities and it was with him that
the U. S. government negotiated the important Fort Laramie
Treaty in 1868. Looked upon with suspicion by his own people
because of his personal ambition and his dealings with the
whites — and with suspicion by the whites as a matter of policy —
Red Cloud was forced always to maintain a position of unpopular
compromise with respect to the important matters that faced the
Sioux nation. He spent the last years of his life as a "Hang-
Around-the-Fort Indian" trying to satisfy both the whites and his
own tribe without antagonizing either. In spite of his posture of
compromise, Red Cloud remained an important figure in that he
tried always to stem the erosion of Sioux culture. Some historians
have pointed out that Red Cloud, perhaps more than any other
Native American leader, exemplified the U.S. government's

misunderstanding of Indian society and the grave difficulties faced by Indians when they were forced to abandon their traditional ways and take up those of the invading white culture.

George Armstrong Custer (1839-1876)

Although he was graduated from West Point at the bottom of his class, Custer quickly gained the attention of his superiors by means of his reckless bravery and crass showmanship in cavalry fights. Custer's promotion, at the young age of twenty-four, to brigadier general is thought by some historians to have been the result of a mistake by an overworked clerk. Nevertheless, flamboyant and successful throughout the Civil War, Custer saw the end of that conflict as the youngest major general in the army. With the coming of peace, the young officer's rank was reverted to that of regular army captain. Soon, however, he was appointed to the rank of lieutenant colonel and sent in command of the newly formed 7th Cavalry to fight Indians on the Great Plains. Custer proved a harsh leader and, as a result, was court-martialed and relieved of his command for a period of months. Later reinstated, Custer led his troops against Black Kettle's Cheyenne camp at the Washita River in Oklahoma in the winter of 1868. When Custer and his troops were wiped out in 1876 at the Little Bighorn, the place the Sioux called "the Greasy Grass," much of America was stunned and angered. After all, Custer was a "winner" — a patriotic hero — and his defeat did not set well with the established powers, as evidenced by the massacre carried out at Wounded Knee in 1890 by Custer's old regiment, the 7th Cavalry.

Crazy Horse (1842-1877)

Tashunca-uitco was this famous Oglala Sioux chief's name — a better translation might be, "His Horse Was Crazy." Crazy Horse was a great warrior who had been active in the campaigns of Red Cloud against the forts and settlements in Wyoming in the period from 1865 to 1868. In 1876 Crazy Horse's force of twelve hundred Oglala and Cheyenne were attacked on the Rosebud River by an army of thirteen hundred troops under the command of General George Crook, whom the Sioux called "Three Stars." Crook was considered by General William Sherman to be the greatest Indian fighter the army ever had. After a day's battle with Crazy Horse, General Crook retreated in defeat. Crazy Horse went on to join Sitting Bull and Gall to defeat Custer at the Little Bighorn, and then to engage the army of General Nelson A. Miles. When Crazy Horse surrendered in May, 1877, he was the last of the important chiefs — except for Sitting Bull and Gall, who had fled to Canada — to do so. In September of that same year, Crazy Horse left the reservation without authorization. He was arrested and taken to jail, where, in a struggle during which he was restrained by his old friend, Little Big Man, Crazy Horse was killed by a white soldier's bayonet. His body was taken by his family to an undisclosed site on or near the Pine Ridge reservation. Crazy Horse never permitted his photograph to be made, and his final resting place remains a mystery.

John M. Chivington (1821-1894)

A Methodist minister and Sunday school teacher, Chivington refused a commission as an army chaplain during the Civil War, opting, he said, for a "fighting" commission rather than a "praying" one. While Colonel Chivington commanded the Union Army forces that defeated the Confederates at Glorieta Pass near Santa Fe, New Mexico, and then drove the southern army from the state, history will best remember him as the racist leader of the Colorado Volunteers who massacred old Cheyenne men, women, and children and then mutilated their corpses at Sand Creek in 1864.

Sitting Bull (1831-1890)

Chief of the Hunkpapa band of Sioux, *Tatonka-Iyotake*, or Sitting Bull, was an outstanding warrior, a revered spiritual leader, and a wily politician. Moreover, he possessed the gift of eloquence and used his talents as long as he could to resist every attempt by the U.S. government to take away Sioux lands. Sitting Bull was reported to have been present at Rosebud Creek when Crazy Horse turned back General Crook's army (accounts differ), and he was most certainly among the Sioux at Custer's defeat at the Little Bighorn. It is interesting that, while the particulars of Custer's death are not certain, Sitting Bull's nephew, White Bull, believed that it was he who had slain the yellow-haired general that day on the Greasy Grass. In the aftermath of Little Bighorn, Sitting Bull and his band traveled north to Canada, where they were to remain for the next four years.

When he returned to the United States in 1881, Sitting Bull surrendered to Major David Brotherton at Fort Buford. The chief spent the next two years as a prisoner and then, in a bizarre twist, he was taken on tour across the country in a Wild West Show — first with a man named Allen and later with Buffalo Bill Cody — and billed as the "Slayer of General Custer." When the Ghost Dance craze swept across the Sioux Nation, Sitting Bull listened and learned about it but remained unconvinced that it was as powerful as its true believers imagined. White authorities, however, believed that Sitting Bull was behind much of the strange new religion and thought it a real threat to whites. Indian Agent James McLaughlin sent a party of forty Sioux Indian police, under the command of Lieutenant Henry Bull Head, to arrest the chief. When Sitting Bull resisted, one of his followers fired a rifle and wounded Bull Head, who, in turn, shot Sitting Bull. In the melee that followed, Sergeant Red Tomahawk drew his pistol and fired a bullet into Sitting Bull's head, killing him. Six policemen and eight of Sitting Bull's followers — including his seventeenyear-old son Crowfoot — were killed in the fight. Sitting

Bull's body was taken away by the surviving police, placed in a homemade coffin filled with quicklime, and buried in the military cemetery at Fort Yates.

Ira Hayes (1923-1955)

Ira Hayes was born on the Pima reservation in Arizona. As a Marine in World War II Hayes was one of the soldiers

Navajo Code Talkers with the Marines on Saipan in 1944. (National Archives)

immortalized in the famous statue of the raising of the American flag on Iwo Jima. Hailed as a hero and displayed across the United States in the war bond effort, Hayes was promoted as a model "good Indian" and was wined and dined and decorated for a period of time. Soon, however, he was forgotten and wandered home to the Pima Reservation where he had no job, no money, and, most importantly perhaps, no Indian culture to sustain him. Having been proclaimed a hero far out of proportion to the courage of his deed, he soon fell victim to the scourge of reservation life: alcoholism. At the age of thirty-two, Ira Hayes was found dead in an irrigation ditch — a drunken Indian drowned in two inches of water.

Wilma Mankiller (1946-   )

The first woman elected to the office of Principal Chief of the Cherokee Nation, Mankiller had been serving as Deputy Chief when former Chief Ross Swimmer was appointed Director of the Bureau of Indian Affairs in 1985. Elected in July, 1987, Mankiller — a former social worker and activist in the Native American Rights movement of the 1960s — oversees the 108,000 member tribe (second only to the Navajo tribe in numbers) and an annual budget that exceeds $52 million.

While history tells us that Indian people have long stood and fought against those who would rob them of their culture, their lands, and even their lives, it is important that we know that in more modern, informed times, Native American men and women are distinguishing themselves in areas other than that of traditional leadership. Areas like art and literature:

Maria Tallchief (1925-   ), one of America's greatest ballerinas — prima ballerina with the American Ballet Theatre — is an Osage from Oklahoma.

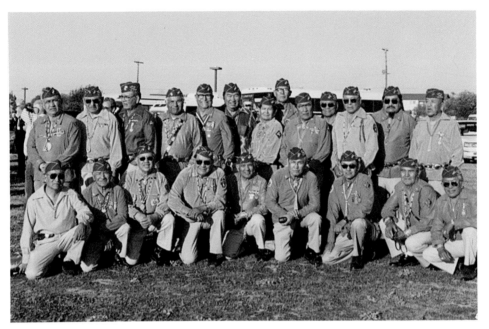

Navajo Code Talkers at a 1987 reunion to commemorate the World War II landing on Iwo Jima. (Department of Defense/Still Media Records Center)

Lynn Riggs (1899-1954) was a Cherokee playwright whose *Green Grow the Lilacs* was made into the classic musical, *Oklahoma*.

N. Scott Momaday (1934-   ) is a Kiowa/Cherokee artist and writer, born in Lawton, Oklahoma, who has taught at the University of California at Berkeley, the University of California at Santa Barbara, Stanford University, and at the University of Arizona, where he is today a professor of English. Momaday has received numerous awards for his work, including a John Jay Whitney Foundation Fellowship, a Guggenheim Fellowship, and a Fulbright Fellowship. In 1969 he received the Pulitzer Prize for his first novel, *House Made of Dawn*.

R. C. Gorman (1931-   ) is a Navajo artist born and raised on the Navajo reservation near Chinle. He has been called the most recognized living American artist and his work is known and appreciated worldwide. R. C.'s father, **Carl Gorman** (1907-   ), himself an acclaimed artist, was a member of the famous Navajo Code Talkers during World War II.

Paula Gunn Allen (1939-   ), who describes herself as a Laguna/Sioux/Lebanese American, is the author of what has been called the first feminist novel by a Native American woman: *The Woman Who Owned the Shadows* (1983).

Leslie Marmon Silko (1948-   ), a Laguna Pueblo, is an acclaimed poet and novelist and the recipient of a MacArthur Foundation Fellowship.

Tony Hillerman (1925-   ) is the author of the popular Jim Chee/Joe Leaphorn detective novels set on the Navajo reservation. While Hillerman is not himself an Indian, his books have perhaps done more to introduce traditional Navajo lifeways to non-Indians than any other source to date.

10 Time Line

43,000 B.C.	Earliest ancestors of Native American people believed to have begun their migration from Asia across land bridge where the Bering Straits are today
1492	Columbus makes landfall in Bahamas
1493	First battle between Native Americans and Europeans
1507	Western Hemisphere first called "America"
1540-1542	Coronado explores the interior of the Southwest
1541-1542	De Soto travels through Arkansas and Oklahoma
1598	Oñate plants settlements in northern New Mexico
1607	Colonists settle in Jamestown, Virginia
1609	Founding of Santa Fe, New Mexico
1610	Virginia colonists wage war on native people
1620	Pilgrims organize Plymouth, Massachusetts
1622	Powhatan Indians attack Jamestown; colonists offer poisoned wine to Indians at peace talks
1637	Pequot War results in virtual extermination of that tribe
1675-1677	King Phillip War, Wampanoag and Narragansett tribes

1676	Wampanoag Chief Metacom ("King Phillip") beheaded
1680	Pueblo Revolt, Indians drive Spaniards from New Mexico; Westo Tribe wiped out in South Carolina
1685	British report that Powhatan Tribe is extinct
1692	De Vargas begins reconquest of New Mexico
1711	Tuscarora War in North Carolina
1715-1727	Creek and Yamasee Tribes engage Carolinian colonists in twelve-year Yamasee War
1763	Ottawa Chief Pontiac and his confederacy capture ten British forts in Ohio River Valley
1774	Delaware, Wyandot, Cayuga Iroquois, and Shawnee defeated in Lord Dunsmore's War in West Virginia
1830	Andrew Jackson's Removal Bill becomes law; Treaty of Dancing Rabbit Creek
1831-1834	Choctaw Tribe forcibly removed from their ancestral homeland in Mississippi to Oklahoma
1837	Mandan Tribe wiped out by smallpox
1838	Cherokee removal over the Trail of Tears
1849	Bureau of Indian Affairs established
1854	First novel by Native American author: *The Life and Adventures of Joaquin Murieta* by John Rollin Ridge
1857	Meadow Mountains Massacre
1861-1865	Civil War
1862	Thirty-eight Sioux leaders hanged at Mankato, Minnesota

1864	Massacre of 133 Indians — most of them women and children — at Sand Creek, Colorado; Kit Carson attacks Navajos at Canyon de Chelly and marches twenty-four hundred survivors to internment camp at Fort Sumner, New Mexico
1867	Custer attacks Black Kettle's camp at the Battle of the Washita in Oklahoma
1871	Camp Grant Massacre near Tucson — over one hundred Indians killed, all but eight of them women and children
1876	Custer and his 7th Cavalry wiped out at the Battle of the Little Bighorn
1877	Defeat of Chief Joseph and the Nez Perce
1883	First autobiography and tribal history by Native American woman: *Life Among the Paiutes* by Sarah Winnemucca Hopkins
1886	Geronimo surrenders
1887	Dawes Severality Act attempts to "Americanize" Indians with allotments of land
1889	Ghost Dance sweeps across the Sioux reservation
1890	Sitting Bull killed by Indian police attempting to arrest him; Big Foot and his band massacred at Wounded Knee
1907	Indian Territory is joined with Oklahoma Territory to become the state of Oklahoma in spite of the government's promises that Indian lands would always remain sovereign
1924	Congress grants citizenship to Indians
1934	Indian Reorganization Act revises the Dawes Act of 1887

1945	First Atomic bomb detonated in New Mexico
1953	House Concurrent Resolution 108 establishes policy of termination of Indian tribes
1964	Civil Rights Act
1968	Civil Rights Act
1969	N. Scott Momaday, a Kiowa, wins the Pulitzer Prize for his first novel, *House Made of Dawn*
1969-1971	Indians seize and hold Alcatraz Island in San Francisco Bay as protest
1970	Organization of National Indian Youth Council
1972	Large-scale protest movement among Indian people
1973	Shoot-out between AIM and FBI near Wounded Knee, South Dakota
1975	Indian Self-Determination and Educational Assistance Act
1987	Wilma Mankiller first woman to be elected Principal Chief of the Cherokee Nation
1992	Native American People protest the five-hundred year anniversary of the "discovery" of America by Columbus

11 Bibliography

Black, Sheila. *Sitting Bull and the Battle of the Little Bighorn.* Englewood Cliffs, New Jersey: Silver Burdett Press, 1989. The story of *Tatanka Yotanka* ("The Sitting Bull"), the brave and resourceful chief and holy man of the Hunkpapa Sioux. This book is one in the Young Adult Biography Series of American Indians

Brown, Dee. *Bury My Heart at Wounded Knee.* New York: Holt, Rinehart and Winston, 1974. Subtitled "An Indian History of the American West," this is a classic work presenting the Indian side of the "winning of the West."

Carter, Forrest. *The Education of Little Tree.* Albuquerque: University of New Mexico Press, 1976. A warm and moving story of a boy, orphaned at five, who goes to live with his Cherokee grandparents.

Cwiklik, Robert. *King Phillip and the War With the Colonists.* Englewood Cliffs, New Jersey: Silver Burdett Press, 1989. Another volume in the Young Adult Biography series, this is the story of *Metacom*, chief of the Wampanoag whom the colonists called "King Phillip," and his attempts to drive the European settlers back across the sea.

Debo, Angie. *And Still the Waters Run: The Betrayal of the Five Civilized Tribes.* Norman: University of Oklahoma Press, 1984. The white government made solemn treaties with the Choctaw, Chickasaw, Cherokee, Creeks, and Seminoles — treaties that were to endure "as long as the waters run." This book details the destruction of the Indian republics.

Deloria, Vine. *Behind the Trail of Broken Treaties: An Indian Declaration of Independence.* Austin: University of Texas

Press, 1985. An account of the events leading to the 1973 occurrence at Wounded Knee and the Indian struggle for political recognition in the years since.

Gordon-McCutchan, R. C. *The Taos Indians and the Battle for Blue Lake*. Santa Fe: Red Crane Books, 1991. Recounts the story of the Taos Indians' successful fight to recover their sacred Blue Lake from the hands of the U.S. government.

Hogan, Linda. *Mean Spirit*. New York: Atheneum, 1990. Novel by a Chickasaw woman, the story tells of the tragic events that came to Indian people in Oklahoma when oil was discovered under their land in the 1920s.

Jones, Douglas. *Arrest Sitting Bull*. New York: Scribner's, 1977. An historical novel about Sitting Bull and the Ghost Dance phenomena.

_____. *The Court-Martial of George Armstrong Custer*. New York: Scribner's, 1976. This novel examines what might have happened if Custer had survived his "last stand" at the Little Bighorn.

Koning, Hans. *Columbus: His Enterprise: Exploding the Myth*. New York: Monthly Review Press, 1991. The subtitle to this short revisionist work is "Exploding the Myth." Describes Columbus as a man consumed by a lust for gold and how his "discovery" led to plunder and murder of native peoples of the Americas.

Lafferty, R. A. *Okla Hannali*. Norman: University of Oklahoma Press, 1972. A wonderful epic novel of Choctaw Indian life in Indian Territory, Oklahoma, this book parallels accurately the history of the Choctaw in the nineteenth century.

Matthiessen, Peter. *In The Spirit of Crazy Horse*. New York: Viking, 1983. A detailed and controversial examination of the events surrounding the shoot-out between FBI agents and members of the American Indian Movement near Wounded Knee, South Dakota, in 1975.

Momaday, N. Scott. *The Names: A Memoir*. Tucson: University of Arizona Press, 1976. Autobiography is mixed with tribal stories in this beautifully written memoir by Kiowa poet, artist, and Pulitzer Prize-winning novelist N. Scott Momaday.

Otis, D. S. *The Dawes Act and the Allotment of Indian Lands*.
Norman: University of Oklahoma Press, 1973. Detailed
account of the Act of 1887 and its consequences up to 1900.

Shorto, Russell. *Geronimo and the Struggle for Apache Freedom*.
Englewood Cliffs, New Jersey: Silver Burdett Press, 1989 The
life of famous Apache medicine man; another volume in the
Young Adult Biography series.

_____. *Tecumseh and the Dream of an American Indian
Nation*. Englewood Cliffs, New Jersey: Silver Burdett Press,
1989. This volume in the Young Adult Biography Series, tells
of the Shawnee leader Tecumseh and his plan to unite the
tribes into an Indian State.

Swan, Brian and Arnold Krupat, editors. *I Tell You Now:
Autobiographical Essays by Native American Writers*. Lincoln:
University of Nebraska Press, 1987. These essays (by eighteen
Native American writers) detail struggles for self-identity and
a sense of self-worth in a world caught between two cultures.

Time-Life Books, with text by Benjamin Capps. *The Great
Chiefs*. Alexandria, Virginia: Time Life Books, 1975. A
volume in the Old West series, this is a fascinating history
with many good photographs and illustrations.

Welch, James. *Winter in the Blood*. New York: Harper & Row,
1974. An important novel by a Blackfeet/Gros Ventre author
describing the tragedy of contemporary reservation experience.

12 Media
Materials

Myths and Moundbuilders (1981). PBS Home Video. The American Experience Series, 58 minutes. An important look at the mysteries left behind by the earliest Native Americans. This film is especially interesting in that it points out the racism behind the long-held notion that Native American people were not sophisticated enough to have constructed the mounds, which have been attributed to a "lost" civilization of highly intelligent and advanced white people.

Geronimo and the Apache Resistance (1988). PBS Home Video. The American Experience Series, 60 minutes. The story of the legendary medicine man's bitter struggle to resist white domination over his people.

Seasons of the Navajo (1984). PBS Home Video. The American Experience Series, 60 minutes. Portrait of a year in the life of a traditional Navajo family working to uphold the ancient culture of the tribe.

The Spirit of Crazy Horse (1990). PBS Home Video. The American Experience Series, 60 minutes. Lakota Sioux Milo Yellow Hair narrates the history of the Sioux of South Dakota from their buffalo-hunting days to the present.

Winds of Change: A Matter of Choice (1989). PBS Home Video. The American Experience Series, 60 minutes. Nez Perce/

German television journalist Hattie Kauffman narrates this look at the choices faced by today's Native American people—whether to live according to traditional lifeways or those of the greater white culture, where "Indian identity grows stronger in the face of discrimination." Includes rare glimpses of life today on Hopi Second Mesa, where photography is strictly banned.

Winds of Change: A Matter of Promises (1990). PBS Home Video. The American Experience Series, 60 minutes. Narrated by Kiowa writer and artist N. Scott Momaday. The Pulitzer Prize-winning novelist examines the plight of Native people today.

Soldier Blue (1970). Embassy Home Entertainment, 105 minutes. Based partly on the tragic Sand Creek Massacre in Colorado, the film includes graphic scenes of the brutal murders of Indian women and children in an early Hollywood effort to show the Indian side of history.

Little Big Man (1971). Key Video, 149 minutes. Dustin Hoffman as a white man raised by Indians who was present at the battle at the Little Bighorn and knew Custer to be a brutal madman.

Ulzana's Raid (1972). MCA Home Video, 103 minutes. Indians' savagery is shown to be a part of their cultural beliefs while the equally savage actions of the white soldiers are clearly evidence of their brutal racism.

Buffalo Bill and the Indians: or Sitting Bull's History Lesson (1976). Key Video, 135 minutes. The film portrays Buffalo Bill as a drunken showman in his "Wild West Show" and Sitting Bull as the real and noble man of the West. In the end, sadly true to history, Sitting Bull has been killed and the "show" goes on to the wild approval of the audience.

Dances With Wolves (1990). Orion Home Video, 181 minutes. Highly entertaining and popular portrayal of Plains Indians, the film is perhaps a little too romanticized, but still presents a more honest and accurate view than most popular motion pictures on the subject.

Son of the Morning Star (1991). Republic Pictures Home Video, 183 minutes. Based on Evan S. Connell's fine 1984 chronicle of Custer and the Little Bighorn, the film is more accurate than most earlier portrayals of Custer and Crazy Horse.

13 Resources

American Indian Law Center
P. O. Box 4456, Station A
Albuquerque, New Mexico 87196
(505) 277-5462
   Founded in 1970, AILC's purpose is to render services, primarily in the fields of research and training, of a broad legal nature.

American Indian Movement
710 Clayton Street, Apt. 1
San Francisco, CA 94117
(415) 566-0251
   Founded in 1968, AIM seeks to encourage self-determination among American Indian people and to establish international recognition of American Indian treaty rights.

Indian Rights Association
1601 Market Street
Philadelphia, PA 19103
(215) 665-4523
   IRA was founded in 1882 to act as a clearinghouse for appeals of all sorts for aid to Indians and for information on all phases of Indian affairs. It further acts to protect the legal and human rights of Native Americans and to promote their welfare.

Indian Youth of America
P.O. Box 2786
Sioux City, Iowa 51106
(800) 828-4492

Founded in 1978 to improve the lives of Indian children, and to inform families, social service agencies, and courts on the rights of Indian people under the Indian Child Welfare Act.

Institute of American Indian Arts
P.O. Box 20007
Santa Fe, New Mexico 87504
(505) 988-6463
IAIA was founded in 1962 in an effort to afford learning opportunities in the arts and crafts to Native American youth.

International Indian Treaty Council
710 Clayton Street, No. 1
San Francisco, CA 94117
(415) 566-0251
IITC was formed in 1974 to draw international attention to Indian problems and Indian rights.

National Congress of American Indians
900 Pennsylvania Avenue, S.E.
(202) 546-9404
NCAI was founded in 1944 to protect, conserve, and develop Indian land, mineral, timber, and human resources; serve legislative interests of Indian tribes; and improve health, education, and economic conditions.

National Indian Youth Council
318 Elm Street, S.E.
Albuquerque, New Mexico 87102
(505) 247-2251
Founded in 1961, NIYC seeks to provide young Indian people with a working knowledge of how best to serve and understand their tribal communities and take advantage of existing educational resources.

Native American Rights Fund
1506 Broadway

Boulder, Colorado 80302
(303) 447-8760

NARF was founded in 1970 to represent Indian individuals and tribes in legal matters of national significance.

Navajo Code Talkers Association
P.O. Box 1395
Gallup, New Mexico 87301
(505) 722-2228

NCTA was founded in 1971 to represent Navajos who served as communicators or "code talkers" in the Marine Corps during World War II. The group promotes the welfare of the Indian veteran in general, and sponsors scholarships for Navajo boys to the Marine Military Academy at Harlingen, Texas.

North American Indian Women's Association
P.O. Box 805
Eagle Butte, SD 57625
(605) 964-2136

Founded in 1970, NAIWA is an educational organization promoting intertribal communication.

Survival of American Indians Association
7803-A Samurai Drive, S.E.
Olympia, Washington 98503
(206) 456-2567

Founded in 1964, SAIA provides public education on Indian rights and tribal government reform action.

NATIVE AMERICANS STRUGGLE FOR EQUALITY

INDEX

Ward, William, 45
Wayne, John, 16, 62
Westo Tribe, 34, 85
White Antelope, 16, 36
Winds of Change: A Matter of Choice, 91
Winds of Change: A Matter of Promises, 92

Woman Who Owned the Shadows, The (Allen), 83
Wounded Knee, 17, 34, 37-39, 40, 68, 77, 86, 87
Wovoka, 16
Wyandot, 34, 85

Yamasee War, 34, 85